The Thirty-nine Steps

JOHN BUCHAN

Level 3

Retold by Roland John
Series Editors: Andy Hopkins and Jocelyn Potter

Pearson Education Limited
Edinburgh Gate, Harlow,
Essex CM20 2JE, England
and Associated Companies throughout the world.

ISBN: 978-1-4058-6234-9

First published in the Longman Structural Readers Series 1966
by arrangement with Messrs William Blackwood & Sons Ltd
This adaptation first published by Addison Wesley Longman Limited
in the Longman Fiction Series 1996
First published by Penguin Books 1999
This edition published 2008

3 5 7 9 10 8 6 4 2

Typeset by Graphicraft Ltd, Hong Kong
Set in 11/14pt Bembo
Printed in China
SWTC/02

Published by Pearson Education Ltd in association with
Penguin Books Ltd, both companies being subsidiaries of Pearson Plc

For a complete list of the titles available in the Penguin Readers series please write to your local
Pearson Longman office or to: Penguin Readers Marketing Department, Pearson Education,
Edinburgh Gate, Harlow, Essex CM20 2JE, England.

Contents

Introduction

A man was standing outside. He was a thin man with a brown beard and small blue eyes. I did not know his name, but he had a flat on the top floor of the building.

'Can I speak to you?' he asked. 'May I come in for a minute?'

I invited him in and shut the door. He seemed very nervous.

'I'm very sorry,' he said. 'But I'm in trouble. Will you help me?'

Richard Hannay has just returned to London from Rhodesia, in Africa. One day he receives a mysterious visit from one of his neighbours, an American newspaper reporter called Scudder. Scudder's life is in danger, and he needs Hannay's help. Hannay enjoys adventure, and he listens with interest to Scudder's story about foreign spies and secret plans. But because he has heard Scudder's story, Hannay's life is in danger too!

Hannay's adventures take him across England to the wild hills of the Scottish Lowlands. The police are looking for him because they think that he is a murderer. Foreign spies are looking for him because he knows their secret plans for war. Can he save his country from a terrible war? He must find a way of telling the top people in the British government about the danger to the country. But first, he must save his own life . . .

The Thirty-nine Steps was written by a Scottish writer, reporter, lawyer and politician, John Buchan (1875–1940). Buchan had a very interesting and exciting life (but not quite as exciting as Richard Hannay's!). He was born in Scotland and went to school in Glasgow. After studying at the universities of Glasgow and Oxford, he worked for a short time as a lawyer. But almost immediately he went into politics, and worked for the British government in South Africa. He returned to London and, in

1907, he married Susan Charlotte Grosvenor.

During the First World War, Buchan was an Intelligence Officer, helping British soldiers to get secret information about their German enemies. He also worked as a reporter for *The Times* newspaper. After the war, he worked as a businessman, and had important jobs in politics and government. He spent parts of his life in South Africa and France. He also lived in Canada, and became the Governor-General there.

He also found time to write more than a hundred books!

Buchan produced many books about history, some of them very long. *Nelson's History of the War* (1915–19), for example, was twenty-four books long. He wrote about the life and work of famous people like Oliver Cromwell, Julius Caesar and Sir Walter Scott. Later, Buchan's readers were able to read about his own life in *Memory Hold-the-Door*. This came out after his death in 1940.

But Buchan is mainly remembered today for his stories of mystery and adventure. His first fictional book was an adventure story in South Africa, *Prester John* (1910). *The Thirty-nine Steps* is the first and the most famous of five spy stories about Richard Hannay. It came out in 1915, while Buchan was working as a reporter during the First World War. *The Thirty nine-Steps* is an exciting spy story with lots of action. Much of this action takes place in the hills of the Scottish Lowlands. Richard Hannay is Buchan's favourite kind of action man: strong, brave and silent. Buchan was thinking about a good friend of his from South Africa, Edmund Ironside, when he was writing about Richard Hannay.

Alfred Hitchcock, the famous film-maker, liked John Buchan's adventure stories very much. In 1935, he made a film of *The Thirty-nine Steps*. He changed a lot of the action, but the main story is the same. There have been other films of the book, but Hitchcock's is the best and the most exciting. Some people think that it is one of the best adventure films ever made.

In his lifetime, Buchan wrote more than thirty fictional books, seven books of short stories and almost a hundred factual works. His last story was *Sick Heart River* (1941).

On 6 February 1940, John Buchan suddenly became very ill while he was shaving. He fell over and badly hurt his head. He died five days later.

Like the work of many popular writers of his time, Buchan's stories became less popular during the 1960s and 1970s. People thought that he was too interested in war. They also thought that his opinions about people from other countries were unacceptable in a modern world. But today there is more interest in his stories. People will always be interested in stories that are exciting and well written. And they will always enjoy reading stories about good, honest people who are not afraid of fighting strong, dangerous enemies – people like Richard Hannay, in Buchan's most popular story, *The Thirty-Nine Steps*.

Chapter 1   The Man Who Died

My name is Richard Hannay and I am thirty-seven years old.

I was born in Scotland, but in 1883 my family moved to Rhodesia. I grew up in Africa and worked hard for 20 years. Then, in March 1914, I returned to Britain. That was five months before the First World War began. I brought a lot of money with me and I wanted to have a good time. Britain was the centre of all my dreams and plans, and I hoped to stay there for the rest of my life.

In May I was living in a flat in London. One evening I was alone there, reading the newspaper. I was interested in a story about Karolides, the Greek Prime Minister.

'He's a good man,' I thought to myself, 'and he's honest too. He's probably the strongest Prime Minister in Europe, and the Germans hate him.'

The sound of the door bell interrupted my reading. I put down the newspaper and opened the door. A man was standing outside. He was a thin man with a brown beard and small blue eyes. I did not know his name, but he had a flat on the top floor of the building.

'Can I speak to you?' he asked. 'May I come in for a minute?'

I invited him in and shut the door. He seemed very nervous.

'I'm very sorry,' he said. 'But I'm in trouble. Will you help me?'

'Well, I'll listen to you,' I said. 'But I can't promise more than that.'

I mixed a strong drink for him and he drank it quickly. When he put down the glass, he broke it.

'Sorry,' he said. 'I'm rather nervous tonight and there's a good reason for that. Now you seem honest, sir. You look like a man who is not easily frightened. Well, I'm in great trouble and I need

1

a good friend.'

'Tell me about it,' I said, 'and then I'll give you my answer.'

'I'm an American,' he said. 'A few years ago I came to Europe to work for an American newspaper. I learned several languages and discovered quite a lot about European politics. I also found out about the German plans for war and I know a group of German spies. Well, these spies are looking for me now, and that's my problem. If you know anything about politics, sir, you'll know this. Europe is very near to war, and there's only one man who can stop it.'

'Who is he?' I asked.

'Karolides, the Greek Prime Minister.'

'Oh, I've just read something about him,' I said. 'There's a story in the evening paper.'

'Yes. Well, the Germans want to kill him,' he said. 'They will kill me too if they can. Karolides is going to come to London next month and he is going to visit the Foreign Office on 15 June. They've chosen that date to kill him. I'm the only man who can save him.'

'And how can I help you, Mr–?'

'Scudder,' he said. 'Franklin P. Scudder. I've just told you, sir, that these spies want to kill me. I thought that I was quite safe from my enemies in London. But yesterday evening I found a card in my letterbox, and there was a man's name on it. It was the name of one of the spies, my worst enemy.'

'You should tell the Foreign Office,' I said. 'They'll help you and perhaps they can save Karolides too.'

'There's no time for that. My enemies know that I'm in this building. They're probably waiting outside. Do you think that I can hide in your flat, sir?'

'Well, I want to check your story first,' I said. 'I'll go outside and look around. If I see anything unusual, I'll agree to help you. Is that all right?'

I left the flat and went out into the street. A man was standing outside the building. He lifted his hand when he saw me. I looked around quickly and saw a face at a window across the street. The man's sign was answered, and the face moved away from the window. I bought another newspaper at the corner of the street and then went back to the flat.

'All right, Mr Scudder,' I said. 'You can stay here tonight. I've checked your story. There's a man outside who is acting rather strangely. I think that your enemies are staying in the house across the street.'

Scudder stayed quietly in my flat for several days. When I went out, he was very nervous. There was always someone standing outside the building. I saw the face at the window opposite mine a few times, but nobody came to the flat. Scudder read and smoked. He filled a little black book with notes, and counted the days to 15 June.

One day he said, 'Time is passing quickly, Hannay. While they're watching the house, I won't be able to get away. If they catch me, will you continue the fight?'

I liked Scudder's adventures, and his story was exciting. But I had no interest in politics. He continued to talk, and I listened to some of it. He told me about a woman by the name of Julia Czechenyi, who was one of the spies. 'She's a terrible enemy, Hannay,' he said, 'but the old man is worse.'

This old man was Scudder's chief enemy, and he described him very clearly. 'It's strange,' he said, 'but he has the voice of a young man. And his eyes, Hannay! When you see his eyes, you never forget them. They're small and often half shut, like the eyes of a bird.'

He talked for a long time that day. I cannot remember everything that he said. But I knew that he was more nervous than usual.

In the evening I went out to dinner with a friend. It was half past ten when I returned. I opened the door of the flat and went in. The lights were not lit and this seemed rather strange. I put them on and looked around. There was nobody there, so I thought that Scudder was already in bed.

I walked into the next room and saw something in the corner. For a moment I could not see what it was. Then I suddenly felt very cold and weak. I wanted to open my mouth and cry out. But I could not move or say anything. Scudder was lying on his back with a knife through his heart.

Chapter 2   The Milkman

I sat down and felt very sick. I sat there for perhaps five minutes and then fear brought me to my feet again. Scudder's white face was too much for me. I covered the body with a tablecloth. I found a drink and sat down again to think. Scudder was dead and his body proved his story. His enemies killed him because he knew their plans.

'They'll kill me next,' I thought. 'They know that he lived on the top floor. They know that he was staying in my flat. And they'll guess that he told me their plans.'

What could I do? Well, I could go to the police and tell them the story. But there was the problem of Scudder's death. 'The police will think that I killed him,' I thought.

I thought about it for a long time and then I formed a plan. I did not know Scudder very well, but I liked him. I enjoyed an adventure too, and I wanted to continue his work.

'I could write to the Prime Minister,' I thought, 'or to the Foreign Office. But perhaps that won't be necessary. I'll go away for a few weeks. Then I'll come back to London and go to the police.'

I went over to Scudder's body and took off the cloth. I

Scudder was lying on his back with a knife through his heart.

searched his pockets for his book of notes, but the book was not there. He had no other papers.

I opened my desk and took out a map of Britain. I thought that Scotland was the best place for my plan. I was born there and I spoke like a Scotsman. I spoke German very well too, and I thought about going to Germany. But perhaps Scotland was a better idea.

I chose Galloway, which was an empty part of the country. There were few big towns there, and it was not too far. I knew that there was a train to Scotland in the morning. It left London at ten minutes past seven. But how could I get out of the flat? Scudder's enemies were probably outside the building, so I had to leave secretly.

Then suddenly I had a great idea. Every morning at half past six the milkman brought my milk. He was a young man and we were the same size. He wore a white hat and coat. My idea was to borrow his clothes and the can of milk. Then I could get away from the building dressed as the milkman.

I went to bed and slept for a few hours. In the morning I counted my money and put fifty pounds in my pocket. While I was getting ready, I remembered my tobacco. I put my fingers into the large tobacco box and felt something hard under the tobacco. It was Scudder's little black book, and I put it in my pocket. It was a good sign, I thought. Scudder hid it there, and his enemies did not find it.

It was twenty minutes to seven now, and the milkman was late. But suddenly I heard the noise of the milk can on the stairs, and I opened the door.

'Come in, please,' I said. 'I want to speak to you.'

He came into the flat, and I shut the door.

'Listen,' I said, 'you're a good man, and I want you to help me.' I took a pound out of my pocket and added, 'If you agree, I'll give you this.'

When he saw the pound, his eyes opened wide.

'What do you want me to do?' he asked.

'I want to borrow your clothes and your milk can for a few minutes,' I said.

He laughed. 'What do you want them for?' he asked.

'I can't explain now. Let me borrow the things, and I'll be back in ten minutes.' I put the pound into his hand.

'All right,' he said. 'I like a bit of fun too.'

I put on his clothes and we went out of the flat. I shut the door behind me.

'Don't follow me,' I said. 'I'll soon be back.'

I went down the stairs and into the street. I made a noise with the milk can and began to sing. A man who was standing outside looked at me. He did not say anything. I looked at the house across the street and saw the face at the window again. I turned into another street and began to run. Then I took off the milkman's clothes and threw them, and the milk can, over a wall.

When I arrived at the railway station, it was ten minutes past seven. The train was moving slowly out of the station, and I had no time to buy a ticket. I ran towards it and caught the handle of a door. I opened it with difficulty and climbed into the train.

The ticket-collector soon came along. He was angry with me, and I had to give him some excuse. But he accepted it and wrote a ticket to Newton-Stewart in Galloway.

Chapter 3   The Innkeeper

All that day I travelled. The train stopped at Leeds station, where I bought some food and the morning newspapers. Another ticket-collector told me that I had to change trains at Dumfries.

I read the papers, but of course there was nothing in them about Scudder's death. It was too early for that. Then I took out Scudder's little book. It was full of numbers, but there were also a few strange names. The words "Hofgaard", "Luneville", "Avocado" and "Pavia" were written there. "Pavia" was there several times.

It was clearly some kind of code, and I am very interested in codes. I thought about this one. I could see that there were numbers in place of letters. But what did the names mean? I knew that some of them were towns. But what code was used for people's names? There is usually a key word in codes like this, and I tried to guess it. "Hofgaard" was clearly not the key word, because it did not fit the rest of the code. I tried the other words too but none of them fitted.

I slept for an hour or two, and then the ticket-collector's voice woke me up.

'Be quick, sir. You have to change here.'

I looked out of the window. We were at Dumfries station. I got out and walked across to the Galloway train.

The train was quite full, and I had an interesting conversation with a farmer. He thought that I was a farmer too! We talked about animals and the price of milk and flour. People got out at different stations, but I continued. At five o'clock the train stopped at a small place and I liked the look of it. I cannot remember its name, but it was quiet. And it was a long way from London.

I left the train and the railway man's child took my ticket. It was a fine evening and I felt quite happy. I followed the road for about a kilometre and then took a path by a river. It was not long before I reached a small house. There was a woman at the door of the house and I spoke to her.

'May I stay here tonight?' I asked.

'You're welcome,' she replied. 'Please come in.'

Very soon she placed a fine meal in front of me, and I drank several glasses of thick, sweet milk.

When it grew dark, her husband came home. He was a big man with thick black hair. We talked for an hour or more, and smoked some of my tobacco. They did not ask me any questions. Perhaps they also thought that I was a farmer.

In the morning I enjoyed a large breakfast. But when I offered a pound to the woman, she refused to take it. It was a warm day, so she gave me a small can of milk to take with me. It was nine o'clock when I left the house.

I walked a few kilometres to the south because I wanted to return to the railway. But of course I could not go back to the same little station. The railway men and the child knew my face. I did not want them to remember me. So I went towards the next station and on my way there I formed a plan. The safest way was to return to Dumfries. If the police were searching for me, I was safer in a big town.

When I reached the station, I bought a ticket to Dumfries. I did not have long to wait until a train came in. I got in with an old man and his dog, and the man soon went to sleep. I borrowed his morning paper, which lay on the seat next to him. The story of the murder was on the first page in big letters: MURDER IN A LONDON FLAT.

The milkman, the paper said, waited for me for half an hour. Then he called the police. They arrived at my flat and found Scudder's body. The milkman was arrested and taken to prison. I felt very sorry for the poor man.

The story continued on the back page. And the latest news

was that the milkman was out of prison. The police were now looking for a man named Richard Hannay! They believed that he was on his way by train to Scotland. I was happy that the milkman was free. He knew nothing about the murder, and he only got a pound for his trouble.

The train stopped at a station which I already knew. It was the place where I got out the night before. Three men were talking to the railway men and the child. I watched them. The child was showing them the road that I took.

The train started again. While it was moving out of the station, I covered my face with the newspaper. It travelled about a kilometre and it suddenly stopped again. We were not at a station. The train was near a bridge over a river. This was my chance, and I changed my plan. I opened the door and jumped out. But the old man's dog tried to follow me. The old man woke up and ran to the door.

'Help! Help!' he cried.

I ran down to the river bank and hid in some long grass there. The ticket-collector and a number of other people were standing at the open door.

A lucky chance saved me. I could now see that the dog was tied to the man. Suddenly the dog jumped out of the train and pulled the old man out too. They fell down the bank, and everybody forgot me for a moment. They picked up the old man, and in the excitement the dog bit somebody. I took my chance and ran away through the long grass.

When I looked back, the excitement was over. People were climbing into the train again, and soon it began to move.

I walked along the river bank and thought about my problem. I was safe but I was also frightened. I do not mean that I was afraid of the police. I was thinking about Scudder's enemies and their plans. I felt sure that they wanted to kill me. Perhaps they wanted to see me in prison. They were a real danger to me, and I felt very frightened. My troubles were not over yet.

The old man's dog tried to follow me.

I climbed up from the river and I reached the top of a hill. There were other hills around me, and I could see clearly for several miles. There was the railway station and one or two houses. A road ran from the station towards the east. Then I looked up into the blue sky, and my heart almost stopped beating. A small plane was flying towards me. And I knew that Scudder's enemies were in that plane. The British police never used planes to look for people.

I hid behind a rock and watched. The plane flew up and down the river bank. It was so low that I could see a man inside. But I was sure that he did not see me. Then it climbed and turned. It flew over the river again and went back to the south. I decided to leave those hills. There was no place for me to hide. And I had no chance against a plane.

At six o'clock I reached the road. I followed it for a few kilometres. It was beginning to get dark when I came to a house standing alone next to a bridge.

A young man was on the bridge reading.

'Good evening,' he said. 'It's a fine evening, isn't it?'

'Yes, it is,' I replied. 'Is this house an inn?'

'Yes, sir, and I'm the innkeeper. Would you like to stay here tonight?'

'You're a very young innkeeper, aren't you?'

'Well, my father died last year and left me this inn. I'm living here with my mother but I don't like the work at all. I prefer to write stories, but what can I write about? I don't meet many interesting people.'

I suddenly had the idea that this young man could help me. 'I'll tell you a story,' I said, 'and it's true too. I need a friend. And I'll tell you this story if you help me. I'll give you permission to write it down, but don't do anything before 15 June. That's a very important date.'

Then I sat on the bridge and told him a story. He listened, and his eyes shone with excitement.

'I'm a farmer from Rhodesia,' I said, 'and I came to Britain a few weeks ago. I travelled by ship from German West Africa. The Germans there thought that I was a spy. They followed me all the way to Britain. They've already killed my best friend, and now they're trying to kill me. Have you read the newspaper today?'

'Yes.'

'Well then, you know about the murder of Franklin Scudder.'

The young man's eyes opened wide.

'He was my best friend, and he was killed in my own flat.'

I told him that Scudder was working for the Foreign Office before his death. And I explained that he told me some of the Germans' secrets. It was quite a long story, and I made it very exciting. At the end I said, 'You're looking for adventure, aren't you? Well, you've found it now. These German spies may come here, and I want to hide from them.'

He took my arm and pulled me towards the inn. 'You'll be safe here, sir,' he said. 'Tell me your adventures again, and I'll write them down.'

'All right. But I have some work to do first. Scudder gave me a long message in code. And I have to find out what it means.'

While we were going into the inn, I heard the plane again. It was flying low towards the bridge.

I had a quiet room at the back of the house. The innkeeper's mother brought me my meals. This place suited me very well.

The next morning I took out Scudder's notebook and began to work. The code was a difficult one, and I had to try many possible key words. By midday I knew where the spaces between the words were. I did not yet know the letters.

After dinner I tried again and worked hard until three o'clock. Then suddenly I had an idea. I was lying back in my chair when a woman's name came into my head. It was Julia Czechenyi, one of Scudder's worst enemies. Perhaps her name was the key word. I tried it quickly on the code and it was right!

"Julia" has five letters, and these letters were used in place of *a, e, i, o* and *u. J* is the tenth letter in English, and so he used the number ten to mean *a*. The letter *e* was the *u* of "Julia", and *u* is the twenty-first letter. So Scudder wrote the number 21 for *e*.

The name "Czechenyi" gave me nine other numbers, and I could soon read Scudder's notes. I sat in my room working quietly all afternoon. The facts in Scudder's little book were terrible. By the time the woman brought my tea, I was a very nervous man. My face looked pale, and I did not want to eat anything.

'Are you all right, sir?' she asked. 'You look ill.'

'Oh, it's nothing,' I said. 'Please put the things on the table.'

There was a sudden noise outside the inn, and the woman left my room. I heard a car stopping and then there were voices downstairs. A few minutes later the innkeeper ran into my room. 'Two men have just arrived,' he said, 'and they're looking for you. They described you very well.'

'What did you tell them?'

'I told them that you stayed here last night but left early this morning.'

'Can you describe them?'

'One is a thin man with dark eyes, and the other is rather fat.'

'Do they talk like Englishmen?'

'Oh, yes, I think so.'

I picked up a bit of paper and wrote quickly in German:

Black Stone. Scudder knew about this, but he could not act until 15 June. Karolides is unsure of his plans, and I probably cannot help. But I will try if Mr T thinks I should

Then I tore the sides of the paper. It looked like part of a private letter.

'Give this to them,' I said. 'Tell them that you found it in my room.'

Three minutes later the men drove away in the car. The innkeeper came back in great excitement.

'Your paper gave them a surprise,' he said. 'The dark one turned pale, and the fat one looked very ugly. They paid for their drinks and left.'

'Now I want you to do something for me,' I said. 'Get on your bicycle and go to the police at Newton-Stewart. Describe the two men and talk about the London murder. You can make something up. You can say that you heard a conversation between them. One man told the other that he was just out of prison. And say that you also heard Scudder's name. It isn't finished yet. Those two men will come back tomorrow morning, and the police have to be here to arrest them.'

He ran for his bicycle, and I continued my work on Scudder's notes. It was six o'clock when he returned.

'It's all right,' he said. 'The police will be here at eight o'clock in the morning.'

We had a meal together, and I had to tell him my adventures again. He made notes about them during the meal. I could not sleep that night. I finished Scudder's book and then sat up in my chair until morning. I was thinking about Scudder's terrible story.

At eight o'clock three policemen arrived at the inn. The innkeeper met them and showed them the garage. They left their car there and then came into the inn.

Twenty minutes later another car stopped a little way from the inn. I was watching from a window above the front door. The car was driven under some trees and left there. Two men got out of it and walked towards the inn.

My plan was not a very good one. I wanted the police to arrest the men. Then I was safe. But now I had a better idea. I wrote a note to the innkeeper and left it in my room. Then I opened my window and dropped quietly into the garden. I ran across the grass and along the side of a field. A few minutes later I reached the trees.

The car was standing there, and I got in. I started it and drove away. The wind carried the sound of angry voices to my ears. But soon I was travelling along that road at 80 kilometres an hour.

Chapter 4   The Adventure with Sir Harry

It was a beautiful morning, but I was not thinking about the fine weather or the views around me. My thoughts were all of Scudder and his notes.

I knew now that Scudder lied to me in my flat. He told me a lot about Karolides, and part of it was true. But he did not tell me his really important secrets. Perhaps he was afraid to tell anyone. Of course Karolides was in danger, but the danger to Europe itself was greater! That was the real secret which Scudder kept in his little book.

The words "thirty-nine steps" were there several times in his notes. In one place he wrote: "Thirty-nine steps. I counted them. High tide 10.17 p.m." What did it mean? The "thirty-nine steps" were somewhere on the coast; the word "tide" proved that. But why were these steps important?

Scudder's notes said that there was definitely going to be a war. Nobody could stop it. The Germans had their plans ready years before, in February 1912. They planned to kill Karolides and to use his death as the excuse for war. "The Germans will talk about calm in Europe," he wrote, "but they're ready for war. They're going to attack us suddenly."

Scudder also wrote about the visit of a French officer to London. He was the head of the French army and was coming

I opened my window and dropped quietly into the garden.

on 15 June. "This officer will learn about the British plans and will then return to France." Scudder added that the Black Stone, the group of German spies, were also going to be in London on that same day. They hoped to learn about the plans too and to send them to Germany. When he died, Scudder was trying to stop them.

I drove on through the pretty villages of Galloway. It was a beautiful part of Scotland. But I could not enjoy the calm that was all around me. I had to get away from my enemies and stop them killing me. I had to find a way to continue Scudder's work. But it was going to be very difficult. The police and the "Black Stone" were after me, and I had no friends in Scotland.

At midday I came to a large village. I was very hungry and I decided to stop there. Then I saw a policeman. He was standing outside the Post Office, reading a telegram.

When he saw my car, he lifted his hand. At the same time he ran into the middle of the road.

'Stop! Stop!' he shouted.

I suddenly knew that the telegram was about me. After their conversation at the inn, perhaps the police accepted the spies' story. The spies probably described me and the car, and the police then sent telegrams to officers in all the villages.

I did not stop. The policeman put out his hand and ran along at the side of the car. He caught my arm through the window, which was open. I hit him very hard and he fell back into the road. I drove into the country again.

I drove up and down several hills. I was tired and hungry. I began to look for a quiet inn where I could rest. But suddenly there was a noise above me and I looked up. The plane was a few kilometres away, flying towards me. I drove fast down a hill between the trees. A car drove out from a side road, and I could not stop. I pulled the wheel hard to the right and shut my eyes.

My car ran through the trees and started to fall. I saw a river

15 metres below me. I jumped out of the car and fell into the grass. There was a terrible noise as the car turned over several times. Then it lay like a pile of old metal on the river bank.

Someone took my hand and pulled me out of the grass. A kind voice said, 'Are you hurt?'

A tall young man was standing there. 'I'm very sorry about this,' he said. 'I saw your car, but neither of us could stop in time. I hope that you're all right. But you look quite pale.'

I was rather pleased about the accident. The police were looking for that car, so I could not travel far in it now.

'I was the one who was driving badly, sir,' I said. 'I was going too fast on these narrow roads. Well, I can't drive that car again. This is the end of my Scottish holiday, but at least I'm not dead.'

'I'm very sorry,' he said again. He looked at his watch and continued. 'There's time to go to my house. You can change your clothes and have something to eat there. Where's your case? Is it down there in the car?'

'No. All my things are at an inn 60 kilometres away.' What could I tell him about myself? I did not want to say that I was Rhodesian. My name was in all the newspapers. The police knew that I was from Rhodesia. So I decided to be an Australian. I knew a lot about Australia. Then he could not discover who I was.

'I'm Australian,' I continued, 'and I never carry a lot of clothes with me.'

'An Australian,' he cried. 'Well, I'm the luckiest man in Scotland! You are against Protection, of course.'

'I am,' I answered quickly. But I had no idea what he meant.

'That's fine. The free movement of goods is the best thing for Britain. Well now, you'll be able to help me this evening.' He took my arm and pulled me towards his car.

A few minutes later we reached the house. He took out three or four of his suits and put them on the bed. I chose a dark blue

I jumped out of the car and fell into the grass.

suit and put it on. I also borrowed one of his shirts. Then he took me to the kitchen. There was some food on the table. 'If we don't hurry, we'll be late,' he said. 'Eat something now and take some food in your pocket. When we get back tonight, we'll have a good meal. We have to be in Brattleburn by seven o'clock.'

I had a cup of coffee and some cold meat. The young man stood by the fire and talked.

'You've come just at the right time, Mr– . Oh, excuse me. You haven't told me your name.'

'Twisdon,' I said.

'Ah, Twisdon. Well, I'm in trouble, Mr Twisdon, and I'd like you to help me. There's a meeting tonight at Brattleburn, and I have to make a political speech. I'm standing for Parliament for this part of Galloway, and Brattleburn is my chief town. Well, I had everything ready for the meeting, and Crumpleton – you know, the last Prime Minister – was going to make the main speech. But I had a telegram from him this afternoon. He's very ill and he can't come. That means that I have to make the speech myself.'

'Well, if you want people to vote for you,' I said, 'you should be able to make a speech.'

'Oh, I can make a short speech all right, but ten minutes is quite long enough for me. Now be a good man, Twisdon, and help me. You can tell the meeting all about the free movement of goods and Australia.'

I did not know anything about this, but I needed help too. Perhaps this was a chance.

'All right,' I said. 'I'm not a very good speaker but I'll talk to your friends about Australia.'

We left the house then and drove towards Brattleburn. On the way the young man told me a few things about himself, and one of these facts was very interesting. His father and mother were dead. So he usually lived with his uncle, who was the Chief

Secretary at the Foreign Office. This was exciting news because the Chief Secretary was an important man. I wanted to meet him. I hoped that this young man could do something for me.

We drove through a little town where two police officers stopped the car. They shone lights on our faces, and I felt very nervous. I was afraid that they were going to arrest me.

'I'm sorry, Sir Harry,' one of the officers said. 'We're looking for a stolen car.'

'Oh, that's all right.' Sir Harry laughed. 'My car is too old for anyone to steal,' he said, and we drove on.

It was five minutes to seven when we reached Brattleburn. Sir Harry stopped the car outside the town hall, and we went in. There were about 500 people in the hall. A man stood up and made a short speech. He explained that Mr Crumpleton was ill and could not come. 'But we're very lucky in Brattleburn this evening,' he continued. 'A famous speaker from Australia is here. First, though, we shall listen to the man who is going to receive every vote in Brattleburn.'

Sir Harry then began his speech. He had about 50 pages of notes in his hand and he started to read them. It was a terrible speech, and I felt very sorry for him. Sometimes he looked up from the papers, and then he lost his place. Once or twice he completely forgot where he was. He remembered a few sentences from a book and he repeated them proudly like a schoolboy. His ideas were quite wrong too. He said that the Government was making terrible mistakes; there was no danger from Germany. I almost laughed out loud.

'There's no danger from Germany at all,' he said. 'The Government has imagined it. The Germans just want to be friends, and so we don't need a big army. We're throwing away money on arms and warships.'

I thought about Scudder's little black book. The Germans' plans were ready. They were not interested in being friendly.

I spoke after Sir Harry and talked about Australia. I described the country's politics and its plans and the work of the Government there. People listened very politely and sometimes showed their agreement. But I forgot all about the free movement of goods!

The speakers were thanked at the end of the meeting. Sir Harry and I got into the car again and drove out of Brattleburn.

'That was a fine speech, Twisdon,' he said, 'and they enjoyed it. Now we'll go home and you can have a good meal. I want you to stay at my house tonight.'

After dinner that night we sat by the fire and talked.

'Listen, Sir Harry,' I said. 'I want to tell you something and it's very important. You're a good man, so I won't hide anything from you. You're quite wrong.'

He looked very surprised. 'You mean, in my speech?' he asked. 'Do you mean about the danger from Germany? Do you think they'll attack us?'

'They will probably attack us next month,' I said. 'Now listen to this story. A few days ago a German spy killed a friend of mine in London . . .'

I remember the light from the fire in Sir Harry's room. I lay back in a big chair and told him everything. I repeated all Scudder's notes and I even remembered about the thirty-nine steps and the tide. I described my adventures with the milkman and the police at the inn.

Then I said, 'The police are trying to arrest me for the murder. But I can prove that I didn't kill Scudder. The fact is that I'm afraid of these German spies. They're much cleverer than the police. If the police arrest me, there will be an accident. And I'll get a knife in my heart, like Scudder.'

Sir Harry was looking at me thoughtfully. 'Are you a nervous man, Mr Hannay?' he asked.

I did not answer him in words. I took down a heavy knife

from the wall. I threw the knife up in the air and caught it in my mouth.

'I learned to do that many years ago in Rhodesia,' I said. 'But a nervous man couldn't do it.'

He smiled. 'All right, Hannay. You needn't prove it. I don't know much about politics but I know an honest man. I believe what you've said. Tell me what I can do to help you.'

'Well, your uncle is the Chief Secretary at the Foreign Office and he'll be able to do something. I want you to write a letter to him. Ask him if I can meet him before 15 June.'

'What name shall I say?'

'Twisdon. It's safer to forget the name Hannay.'

Sir Harry sat down at a table and wrote this letter.

Dear Uncle,

I have given your address to a man named Twisdon who wants to meet you. He hopes to see you before 15 June. Be kind to him, please, and believe his story.

When he comes, he'll say the words "Black Stone". And he'll sing a few lines of "Annie Laurie".

'Well, that looks all right,' Sir Harry said. 'My uncle's name is Sir Walter Bullivant, and his house is near Artinswell on the River Kennet. Now, what's the next thing?'

'Can you give me an old suit of clothes?' I said. 'And show me a map of Galloway. If the police come here to look for me, you can show them the car. But don't tell them anything.'

'And if the spies come, what shall I say to them?'

'Say that I've gone to London.'

Sir Harry brought the clothes and a map of Galloway. I looked at the map and found the railway to the south.

'That's the emptiest part of the country,' Sir Harry said, showing me an area not far away. 'Go up the road here and then turn to the right. You will be in the hills before breakfast. You'll be quite safe up there but you'll have to travel south on 12 or 13 June.'

He gave me an old bicycle and at two o'clock in the morning I left his house. At five o'clock the sun came up and I was about 30 kilometres away. Green hills rose around me on every side.

Chapter 5   The Roadman Who Wore Glasses

I rested for a time on the top of a hill. The road ran across a flat space in front of me and then down to a river. A small house stood in the fields below, but there were no other signs of life. I was very tired, so I lay down and closed my eyes.

It was seven o'clock when a sound woke me; it was the plane again. I did not move. It flew low over the hills. It turned towards me and I could see the two men in it. Both men were looking at me. I felt sure that they knew me. Then the machine climbed quickly and flew away to the east. I had to get away from that place before they returned. They probably saw my bicycle, so I had to throw it away.

I left the road and pushed the bicycle into some trees. Then I saw a small pool and threw the bicycle into it. The day was warm and clear and I could see the road to the east and the west. There was nothing on it. But I was sure that my enemies were on their way down that road. So I turned across the hills to the north.

After a time I looked back. My eyes are very good, and I saw a line of men walking side by side. There was a space of about 9 metres between one man and the next. They were all coming towards the high ground. I ran but did not get very far. There were more men in front.

'I can't get away from here,' I thought. 'If I move, they'll see me. So I have to stay on the high ground and hide somewhere.'

It was seven o'clock when a sound woke me; it was the plane again.

I ran along the top of the hill and reached the road again. I turned a corner of the road and there I found the roadman. He was preparing for work, but he was moving very slowly. He looked up as I came near.

'This is a terrible job,' he said, 'and I can't do it today. I'm too ill to work, and that's a fact.'

He was a strange-looking man and he wore a pair of large glasses. His eyes looked very red.

'What's the matter?' I asked, but I knew the answer. 'You do this job every day, don't you? Why can't you do it today?'

'I do,' he replied, 'but my daughter doesn't come home from London every day. She came home yesterday, and we had a party last night.' He took off his glasses and then continued. 'I got very drunk last night and my head feels terrible.'

'I'm sorry,' I said. 'Bed is clearly the best place for you.'

'Ah, but it's not easy. My new boss is coming today to see me and my work. If I go home to bed, he won't find me here. And then I'll lose my job.'

Suddenly I had a good idea. 'Listen,' I said. 'Perhaps I can help you. Does the new boss know you very well?'

'No. I don't know him but I know about him. He travels around in a little car.'

'Where's your house?' I asked.

He showed me a small house in the fields below.

'Good. You go back to bed then and get some sleep. I'll do your job. If the boss doesn't know you, he won't know me either.'

He looked at me and then laughed. 'Well, you're a very nice man. It'll be quite easy too and you needn't do much work.'

He showed me a pile of stones. 'I broke up those stones yesterday,' he said, 'and you needn't do any more of that. Go down the road until you come to a pile of rocks. Bring them up here. I'll break them up tomorrow. My name is Alexander Turnbull but my friends call me Specky. That's because I wear these glasses. When the boss comes, you'll have to talk politely. And call him "Sir". He'll be quite happy then.'

'Perhaps the boss knows that you wear glasses,' I said. 'Let me borrow them for today.'

He laughed again. 'Well, well, this is fun.' He gave me his glasses and his dirty old hat.

I took off my coat and gave it to him. 'Take this home with you,' I said, 'and keep it for me.'

Then he left me.

Ten minutes later I looked like a roadman myself. I had put dirt on my trousers and shoes. Turnbull's trousers were tied below the knee, so I tied mine in the same way. Spies look at everything, and I was worried about my hands. They looked clean and rather soft, so I made them dirty.

Turnbull's food and an old newspaper lay on the side of the road. It was eight o'clock now, and I was feeling quite hungry. So I stole some of his bread and cheese and had a quick meal.

Then I began my new job and carried the rocks up the road. While I was working, I remembered an old friend in Rhodesia. He was a policeman when I knew him. His life was strange and difficult. When he was in danger, he often dressed as another person. He told me, 'But clothes alone aren't enough, Hannay. You have to try to *be* another person and you have to believe it yourself. If you can't do that, you will fail.'

So now I believed that I was the roadman. And I thought about my life and my job. I lived in the little house below. My daughter came home yesterday and we had a party. I got drunk and was feeling sick. But the new boss wanted to see me today, and I had to wait for him.

I worked for an hour or more and got quite dirty. It was a very dirty job. Suddenly a voice spoke from the road and I looked up. A young man was talking to me from a small car.

'Are you Alexander Turnbull?' he asked. 'I'm your new boss,

and my office is in the town hall at Newton-Stewart. The road looks all right here, Turnbull. There's a soft part about a kilometre away, and you should clean the sides of the road. I'll be around here again next week. Good morning.'

He drove away, and I felt very happy. My acting was quite good enough for him.

At about eleven o'clock a farmer drove some sheep down the road. When he saw me, he stopped.

'Where's Specky?' he asked.

'He's ill,' I replied. 'I'm doing his job for a few days.'

At about midday a big car came down the road. It went past me and stopped about a hundred metres away. Three men got out of the car and walked slowly back towards me. I knew two of them. They were the men who visited the Galloway inn. One of them was thin and dark and the other was rather fat. But I did not know the third man, who was older than the others.

'Good morning,' the third man said. 'You have a nice easy job here.'

I took my time. I put down a large rock and stood up slowly. They were watching me, and their eyes missed nothing.

'There are worse jobs than this,' I said, 'but there are probably better ones too. I'd like to have yours and sit all day in that big car.'

The elder man was now looking at Turnbull's newspaper.

'Do you get the papers every day?' he asked.

'Yes, I get them but they're three or four days late.'

He picked up the paper and looked at the date on it. Then he put it down again. The thin one was looking at my shoes and spoke a few words in German.

Then the older man said, 'You have a fine pair of shoes. Did you buy them here?'

'I did not,' I said. 'These shoes came from London. I got them from the gentleman who was shooting here last year. Now what

Three men got out of the car and walked slowly back towards me.

was his name?' And I tried to remember the name.

The fat man now spoke in German. 'Let's go,' he said. 'This man is all right.'

They asked me one more question. 'Did anyone go past here early this morning? Perhaps he was riding a bicycle.'

I thought about this question for a moment. Then I said, 'Well, I was a bit late this morning. My daughter came home from London yesterday and we had a party last night. I left the house at about seven o'clock, and there was nobody on the road then.'

The three men said goodbye to me and went back to their car. Three minutes later they drove away. I felt very happy, but I continued to work. It was good that I did, too; the car soon returned. The three men looked at me again as they went past.

I finished Turnbull's bread and cheese and by five o'clock the work was completed. But I was not sure about the next step. I felt sure that my enemies were staying in the area. I decided to go down to Turnbull's house. I could take his things back to him and get my coat. I could stay there until it was dark. And then I hoped to get away across the hills.

But suddenly another car came down the road and stopped. There was one man in it and he called to me.

'Have you got a light?'

I looked at him and knew him. This was a very lucky chance. His name was Marmaduke Jopley, and I saw him once or twice in London before the murder. I hated the man. He was a friend of rich young men and old ladies who often invited him to their homes. Well, Jopley was too weak to hurt me. I decided to act quickly.

'Hullo, Jopley,' I said. 'I'm surprised to see you here.'

His face grew pale. 'Who are you?' he asked in a nervous voice.

'Hannay,' I said. 'From Rhodesia. Don't you remember me?'

31

'Hannay the murderer!' he cried.

'That's right. Now listen to me. If you don't do this quickly, I'll be Jopley's murderer too. Give me your coat and hat.'

He was very frightened. He did what I told him to. I put on his new coat over my dirty clothes and put his hat on my head. Then I gave him Turnbull's glasses and dirty old hat.

'Wear them for a few minutes,' I said. 'Nobody will know you.'

Which way now? Jopley was driving from the east, and I decided to go back that way. I got in the car and ordered Jopley into the passenger seat. Then I drove off.

'Now, Jopley,' I said, 'if you're no trouble, I won't hurt you. But don't try anything and don't talk. Remember that I'm a murderer. If you make any trouble, I'll kill you.'

We drove 13 kilometres along the road. Several men were standing on the corners while we drove past. They looked at the car but did not try to stop us. At about seven o'clock I turned into a narrow road and drove up into the hills. The villages and houses were soon behind us. At last I stopped the car in a quiet place. I gave Jopley his coat and hat and took back Turnbull's glasses and the old hat.

'Thank you,' I said. 'Now you can go and find the police.'

I watched the red light of his car as he drove over the hill.

Chapter 6   The Man with the Strange Eyes

It was a cold night and I was very hungry. Turnbull had my coat, and my watch and Scudder's notebook were in one of its pockets. My money was in the pocket of my trousers. I lay down in some long grass but could not sleep. I thought about all the people who were helping me. And I decided that I was a very lucky man.

Food was my main problem. I closed my eyes and saw thick

pieces of meat on a white plate. I remembered all my past meals in London. There I often refused fruit after dinner! Now an apple was just a dream.

Towards morning I slept a little, but I woke again at about six o'clock. I sat up and looked down the hill. Then I lay back down again in great surprise. Men were searching the long grass below me and they were not far away.

I moved a few feet and hid behind a rock. Then I climbed up behind the rock to the top of the hill. When I reached the top, I looked back again. My enemies were a long way below. I ran over the hill-top to the other side. Nobody could see me there, so I ran for half a kilometre. Then I climbed to the top again and looked down. The men saw me and moved towards me. I ran back over the hill-top and returned to my first hiding place. My enemies were now going the wrong way, and I felt safer.

My best plan was to go to the north, and I chose a good path. Soon there was a river between me and my enemies. But when they discovered their mistake, they turned back quickly. I saw them suddenly above the hill-top, and they began to shout at me. I saw then that they were not my real enemies. Two of them were policemen.

'Jopley has reported me,' I thought, 'and now they're looking for the murderer.'

Two men ran down and began to climb my hill. The policemen ran across the hill-tops to the north. I felt frightened now because these men knew the country. I had strong legs but did not know the best paths.

I left my hill-top and ran down towards a different river. There was a road along the side of it, and there was a gate at the side of the road. I jumped over the gate and ran across a field. The path led through a group of trees. I stopped in the trees and looked back. The police were half a kilometre behind me.

I climbed over a low wall where the trees came to an end. I

There was a glass building at the side of the house, and an old man was sitting at a desk inside.

found myself in a farmyard. The farmhouse was about 30 metres away.

There was a glass building at the side of the house, and an old man was sitting at a desk inside. He looked up at me when I walked towards the building. The room was full of books and cases which contained old pieces of stone and broken pots. I saw several glass cases of old money. Books and papers covered the old man's desk.

He was a kind-looking old man with a round face and not much hair. When I entered, he did not move or speak. I could not say a word either. I looked at him and saw his eyes. They were small and clear and very intelligent. The skin on his head was smooth and shone like a glass bottle.

Then he said slowly, 'You are in a hurry, my friend.'

His eyes followed mine across the farmyard and the field. Some people were climbing over the gate at the road.

'Ah, they're policemen,' he said, 'and you're running away from them. Well, we can talk about it later. I don't want the police to come in here. If you go into the next room, you'll see two doors. Go through the doorway on the left and shut it behind you. You'll be quite safe in there.'

Then he picked up a pen and went on with his work.

I did what he said. I went into the next room and through the left-hand doorway. It was very dark inside. There was only one window, which was high up in the wall. I was safe from the police in that room but I was not very happy. Everything seemed too easy, and I began to think to myself, 'Why did that old man help me? He doesn't know me, and he didn't ask me any questions.'

While I was waiting, I thought about food again. I made plans for my breakfast, and it was very exciting. I wanted eggs. The old man could not refuse to give me some. I was ready for about ten of them. I was thinking about this meal when the door opened. A man who was standing outside made a sign to me. I followed him to the old gentleman's room.

'Have the police gone?' I asked.

'Yes. They asked me if you were here. But I didn't tell them anything important. This is a lucky morning for you, Mr Hannay.'

He spoke quietly and with the voice of a young man. I was watching him all the time. He closed his eyes but they were only half-shut, like the eyes of a bird. And I suddenly remembered Scudder's words. 'If you see his eyes, Hannay, you'll never forget them.' Was this man Scudder's worst enemy? And was I now in the enemy's house? Was it time to kill him? He guessed my plan and smiled. Then his eyes moved to the door behind me. I turned. Two large men were standing there for his protection.

He knew my name but he did not know my face. And this was my only chance.

'What are you talking about?' I asked. 'My name isn't Richard Hannay. It's Ainslie.'

'Is it? But of course you have other names. We won't fight about a name.' He continued to smile at me.

I thought of another plan quickly. I had no coat and my clothes were very dirty. So I began to tell him a story.

'Why did you save me from the police?' I asked. 'I didn't want to steal that money. It has given me a lot of trouble. You can have it.' And I took four pounds from my pocket and threw them on the old man's desk.

'Take it,' I said, 'and let me go.'

'Oh, no, Mr Hannay, I won't let you go. You know too much. You're acting very well but not well enough.'

I couldn't tell if he was sure about me.

'I am not acting,' I said. 'Why don't you believe me? I stole that money because I was hungry. The two men left the car and went away after the accident. I climbed down the bank and found the money on the floor of the car. The police are looking for me, and I'm very tired.'

The old man was clearly not sure now.

'Tell me your adventures,' he said. 'Tell me about yesterday.'

'I can't. I'm really hungry. Give me a meal first, and then I'll tell you everything.'

He made a sign to one of the men, who brought me some cold meat and a glass of milk. Suddenly, while I was eating, the old man spoke to me in German. I did not look up or answer him.

When I finished eating, I began my story again. I was on my way from Leith to visit my brother in Wigtown. I was not travelling by train because I did not have much money. On my way I saw an accident. A car ran off the road. A man jumped out of the car before it fell. And then another man came. They talked for a few moments and then went away together. I climbed down to the car. It was completely destroyed, but I found the four pounds on the floor. I put the money in my pocket and ran away.

I went into a shop in the nearest village and tried to buy some food. I offered a pound to the shopkeeper. She did not like the look of me and called the police. I got away, but the policeman tore my coat off.

'Well,' I cried, 'they can have the money back. A poor man hasn't got a chance.'

'That's a good story, Hannay,' the old man said. 'But I don't believe it.' Then he sat back in his chair and began to play with his right ear.

'It's true,' I shouted. 'My name is Ainslie, not Hannay. Those policemen knew me and were shouting my name from the hill-top.'

I looked at the clear eyes and the shining head in front of me. He was not at all sure. He did not know my face. It was different from my photographs. And my clothes were very old and dirty.

'You'll have to stay here,' he said at last. 'If you aren't Richard Hannay, you'll be quite safe. But if you *are*, I'll kill you myself.'

He pushed a bell and another man came in.

'Bring the car,' he said. 'There'll be three for dinner.'

He looked at me again, and there was something quite terrible in his eyes. They were cold and hard, and very dangerous. I could not look away from them. They made me weak, like a child, and I wanted to go to him. He was Scudder's worst enemy. But for a moment I needed to join him.

He spoke in German to one of the men. And when I heard his words, my strange thoughts left me.

'Karl, put him in the back room and don't let him get away. Remember that,' he said.

The room was very dark, but the two men did not come inside with me. They sat down outside, where I could hear them talking. I felt around the walls of the room and touched several boxes. Then I sat down on one of the boxes to think about my problems.

The old man's friends *did* know my face. They knew me as the roadman, and I was wearing Turnbull's clothes. I could imagine their questions: Why were the police looking for a roadman? Why was he found 30 kilometres away from his job? They probably remembered Marmaduke Jopley too, I thought, and Sir Harry. I could not continue to lie to these foreign enemies and I did not want to be alone with them here. My chances of getting away were not very great.

Suddenly I grew angry and hated these German spies in Britain. I could not sit in this dark place and do nothing. I had to attack them or try to get away.

I got up and walked around the room again. The boxes were too strong for me to open, but then I found a cupboard in the wall. It was probably locked, because I could not open it. But there was a hole in the door. I pushed my fingers into the hole and then pulled hard. The door of the cupboard broke open.

There were some strange things inside. There were bottles and small boxes and some old yellow bags. I found a box of detonators. I took out the detonators and placed them on the floor. At the back of the cupboard I found a strong box. At first I thought that it was locked. But it opened quite easily, and it was full of sticks of dynamite.

I could destroy the house with this dynamite. I often used it in Rhodesia and I knew it well. It could very easily destroy me too! This was clearly a chance to get away, and it was probably my only chance. So I decided to take it.

I found a hole in the floor near the doorway. I pushed a stick of dynamite into the hole and tied a detonator and a long piece of cotton to it. Then I moved one of the boxes until it stood over the hole. I sat down near the cupboard and lit the piece of cotton. I watched the fire as it moved along the cotton. The two men were talking quietly outside the door.

Suddenly there was a terrible noise, and great heat and light came up from the floor. They hung for a moment in the air, and then clouds of dirt took their place. Thick yellow smoke filled the room, and at first I could not see anything. But there was light in the room now from a great hole in the wall. I ran towards it. The air outside was also full of smoke, and I could hear the sound of voices.

I climbed through the hole and ran. I was in the farmyard at the back of the house. About 30 metres away there was a tall stone bird-house. The building had no doors or windows but there were a lot of small holes for the birds. And the roof seemed flat. It looked a good place to hide.

I ran through the smoke to the back of the bird-house. Then I began to climb. It was hard work, and I went up very slowly. But at last I reached the top and lay down behind a low wall. I felt sick from the smoke and very tired. But I was safe up there and soon I fell asleep.

I probably slept for several hours. When I woke up, the

I climbed through the hole and ran.

afternoon sun was very strong. I could hear men's voices again and the sound of a car. I lifted my head a little and looked over the wall. Four or five men were walking across the farmyard to the house. The old man was with them and he was clearly very angry. He shouted something in German to the other men. The thin dark one was there, and the fat one too.

I lay on the roof of the bird-house all afternoon. I was very thirsty. There was a little river next to the farm and I could hear the sound of water. I felt the money in my pocket. Almost no price was too high for a glass of water at that moment!

Two men drove away in the car. A little later another man rode towards the east on a horse. The search was beginning, but they were all going the wrong way. I sat up on the roof and looked around. At first I saw nothing very interesting but then my eyes fell on a large area of trees. These trees were half a kilometre from the house, and they stood around a flat green field.

'That looks like an airfield,' I thought. 'It's a good place for a secret airfield.'

You could not see the field from the ground and a small plane could land there between the trees.

Then I saw a thin blue line far away to the south. It was the sea. So our enemies had this secret airfield in Scotland, and they could watch our ships every day. The thought made me very angry. It made me nervous too. Someone in a plane could easily see me below them. But I could do nothing until it was dark.

I lay and waited on the roof of the bird-house. At about six o'clock a man came out through the hole in my prison. He walked slowly towards the bird-house, and I felt quite frightened for a moment. But then we both heard the plane at the same time. The man turned and went back inside.

The plane did not fly over the house, and I was happy about that. It flew around the trees once and then landed. Some lights shone for a moment or two, and ten minutes later I heard voices.

After that everything was quiet, and it began to grow dark.

I waited until about nine o'clock. Then I climbed down from the roof and reached the ground safely. I moved away from the bird-house on my hands and knees. I went first to the little river. I lay there and drank the cold water. Then I began to run. I wanted to get as far away as possible from that terrible house.

Chapter 7   The Fisherman

I was free now but I felt rather sick. I could smell the smoke of the dynamite and an hour later I had to rest.

It was about 11 o'clock when I reached the road safely. I wanted to go back to Mr Turnbull's cottage. My coat was there, with Scudder's notebook in the pocket, and I had to have that book. My plan then was to find the railway and travel to the south. After that I hoped to go straight to Artinswell to meet Sir Walter Bullivant.

It was a beautiful night. I knew that Turnbull's cottage was about 30 kilometres away. It was too far for me to walk before morning. So I decided to hide during the day and travel only at night.

When the sun rose, I was near a river. I washed in the clean cold water because I was very dirty. My shirt and trousers were torn, and I was afraid to meet anyone in that state. But just the other side of the river I came to a cottage. And I was so hungry that I had to stop there.

The man was not at home, and at first his wife did not like the look of me. She picked up a stick and seemed ready to attack me.

'I've had a bad fall in the hills,' I said, 'and I'm feeling ill. Will you help me?'

She did not ask any questions but invited me into the house. She gave me a glass of milk and some bread and cheese. Then I sat by the fire in her kitchen and we talked. I offered her money for her trouble, but she refused it at first.

'If it isn't your money, I don't want it,' she said.

I grew quite angry. 'But it *is* my money. Do you think that I stole it?'

She accepted it then and unlocked a cupboard in the wall. She gave me a warm piece of Scottish cloth to put over my shoulder and one of her husband's hats. When I left her cottage, I was like a real Scotsman!

I walked for two or three hours. Then the weather changed and it began to rain. But I kept warm and dry under the cloth. A little later I came to a large rock which hung over some low ground. The grass under the rock was quite dry. So I lay down and slept there all day.

When I woke up, it was almost dark. The weather was the same, wet and cold, and I was not sure of the way. Twice I took the wrong path and probably walked more than 30 kilometres. But at six o'clock in the morning I reached Mr Turnbull's cottage.

Mr Turnbull opened the door himself, but he did not know me. 'Who are you?' he asked. 'Why are you coming here on a Sunday morning? I'm just getting ready to go to church.'

I knew nothing about the days of the week; every day seemed the same to me. I felt too ill to answer him. But then he remembered me.

'Have you got my glasses?' he asked.

I took them out of my pocket and gave them to him.

'Of course, you've come back for your coat,' he said. 'Come in, man. You look terrible. Wait. I'll get you a chair.'

When I was in Rhodesia, I was often ill. And one of these African illnesses returned time after time. I knew the signs very well. Soon Mr Turnbull was taking off my clothes and leading me to a bed.

I stayed with him for ten days, and he looked after me very well. The illness lasted about six days. Then my body returned to its usual temperature and I got up.

He went out to work every morning and returned in the evening. I rested all day. He had a cow which gave us milk. And there was always some food in the house.

One evening I said, 'There's a small airfield about 24 kilometres away. Do you know it? A little plane lands there sometimes. Who owns the place?'

'I don't know,' he said. 'I've seen the plane, of course, but I don't know anything about it.'

He brought me several newspapers while I was staying with him. I read them with interest, but I saw nothing about the murder in London. Turnbull did not ask me any questions, not even my name. I was surprised about this, and one day I said, 'Has anyone asked you about me?'

'There was a man in a car,' he said. 'He stopped one day and asked me about the other roadman. That was you, of course. He seemed a very strange man, so I didn't tell him anything.'

When I left the cottage, I gave Turnbull five pounds. He did not want to take the money at all. His face grew red, and he was quite rude to me. 'I don't want money,' he said. 'When I was ill, you helped me. Then you were ill, and I helped you. I can't take such a lot of money.' But he took it in the end.

The weather was beautiful that morning, but I was beginning to feel nervous. It was 12 June, and I had to finish Scudder's business before the 15th. I had dinner at a quiet inn in Moffat and then went to the railway station. It was seven o'clock in the evening.

'What time does the train go to London?' I asked.

'Ten minutes to twelve,' the railway man said.

It was a long time to wait, so I left the station. I found a quiet place near a hill-top and lay down there to sleep. I was so tired that I slept until twenty minutes to twelve. Then I ran down to the station where the train was waiting.

I decided not to go to London. I got out of the train at Crewe and waited there for two hours. The next train took me to Birmingham, and I reached Reading at six o'clock in the evening. Two hours later I was looking for Sir Walter Bullivant's cottage at Artinswell.

The River Kennet ran along next to the road. The English air was sweet and warm, quite different from Scottish air. I stood for a few minutes on a bridge which went across the river. And I began to sing "Annie Laurie" in a low voice.

A fisherman came up from the bank of the river. As he walked towards me, he began to sing "Annie Laurie" too.

The fisherman was a great big man. He was wearing an old pair of grey trousers and a large hat. He looked at me and smiled. And I thought that he had a good and honest face. Then he looked down with me at the water.

'It's clean and clear, isn't it?' he said. 'The Kennet's a fine river. Look at that big fish down there. But the sun has gone now. If you try all night, you won't catch him.'

'Where?' I said. 'I can't see him.'

'Look. Down there. A metre from those water plants.'

'Oh, yes. I can see him now. He's like a big *black stone*, isn't he?'

'Ah,' he said, and sang a few more words of "Annie Laurie".

He continued to look down at the water. 'Your name is Twisdon, I believe,' he said.

'No,' I said. Then I remembered my other names and added quickly, 'Oh, yes, that's right.'

He laughed. 'A good spy always knows his own name,' he said.

Some men were walking across the bridge behind us, and Sir Walter spoke more loudly.

'No, I won't,' he said. 'You're strong enough to work, aren't

45

I stood for a few minutes on a bridge which went across the river.
And I began to sing "Annie Laurie" in a low voice.

you? You can get a meal from my kitchen, but I won't give you any money.'

The men went past, and the fisherman moved away from me. He showed me to a white gate a hundred metres away and said, 'That's my house. Wait here for five minutes and then go around to the back door.'

When I reached his cottage, the back door was open. Sir Walter's butler was waiting to welcome me.

'Come this way, sir,' he said, and he led me up the stairs. He took me into one of the bedrooms. There were clothes on the bed. I saw a dinner-suit and a clean white shirt. But there were other clothes too and several pairs of shoes.

'I hope that these things will fit you, sir,' the butler said. 'Your bath is ready in the next room. You'll hear the bell for dinner at nine o'clock, sir.'

When he left, I sat down. I thought that I was dreaming. At this time the day before I was asleep on a Scottish hill-top. Now I was in this beautiful house, and Sir Walter did not even know my name.

I had a bath and then put on the white shirt and the dinner-suit. Everything fitted me very well. The bell went for dinner, and I hurried down to meet Sir Walter.

'You're very kind, sir,' I said, 'but it is time to tell you about my situation. I haven't done anything wrong, but the police are looking for me at this moment.'

He smiled. 'That's all right. We can talk about these things after dinner. I'm pleased that you got here safely.'

I enjoyed that meal, and the wine was good too. Sir Walter was an interesting man who had travelled in many foreign countries. I talked about Rhodesia and the fish in the Zambesi River, and he told me some of his adventures.

After dinner we went into his library, and the butler brought us coffee. It was a very nice room, with books and fine pictures around the walls. I decided to buy a house like that after I finished Scudder's work.

Sir Walter lay back in his chair.

'I've followed Harry's orders,' he said. 'And now I'm ready to listen, Mr Hannay. You've got some news, I believe.'

I was surprised to hear my real name, but I began my story. And I told him everything. I described my meeting with Scudder and his fears about Karolides. I told him about the murder and my adventure with the milkman.

'Where did you go then?' he asked.

'I went to Galloway. I soon discovered the secret of Scudder's code and then I could read his notes.'

'Have you got them with you?'

'Yes.'

Then I described my meeting with Sir Harry and how I helped him at Brattleburn.

Sir Walter laughed. 'Harry can't make a speech,' he said. 'He's a good man but his ideas are very strange. Please go on with your story, Mr Hannay.'

I told him about Turnbull then and my job as a roadman. He was very interested in that.

'Can you describe those men in the car?' he asked.

'Well, one of them was thin and dark. I saw him before at the inn with the fat one. But I didn't know the third man, who was older than the others.'

'And what did you do after that?'

'I met Marmaduke Jopley next, and had a bit of fun with him.' Sir Walter laughed again when I described that part of the story. But he did not laugh at the old man in the farmhouse.

'How did you get away from the place?' he asked.

'I found dynamite and detonators in a cupboard,' I replied, 'and I almost destroyed the building. There's a small airfield there where the plane lands. After that I was ill for a week. Turnbull looked after me very well. Then I travelled south by train, and here I am.'

Sir Walter stood up slowly and looked down at me.

'You needn't be afraid of the police, Hannay,' he said. 'They aren't looking for you now.'

I was surprised to hear this.

'Why?' I cried. 'Have they found the murderer?'

'No, not yet. But the police know that you didn't kill Scudder.'

'How do they know that?'

'Because I received a letter from Scudder. He did several jobs for me, and I knew him quite well. He was a good spy, but he had one problem.'

'What was that?'

'He always wanted to work alone, and he failed for that reason. The best spies always work with others, but Scudder couldn't do that. I was very sorry about it because he was a fine man. I had a letter from him on 31 May.'

'But he was dead then. He was killed on 23 May, wasn't he?'

'Yes, and he wrote the letter on the 23rd. He sent the letter to Spain first, and then it came back to England.'

'What did he write about?'

'He told me that Britain was in great danger. He also said that he was staying with a good friend. And I believe that the "good friend" was you, Hannay. He promised to write again soon.'

'What did you do then?'

'I went to the police. They knew your name and we sent a telegram to Rhodesia. The answer was all right, so we were not worried about you. I guessed why you left London. You wanted to continue Scudder's work, didn't you? Then I got Harry's letter and I guessed that Twisdon was Richard Hannay.'

I was very pleased to hear all this. My country's enemies were my enemies, but the police were now my friends. And I was a free man again!

Sir Walter sat down and smiled at me.

'Show me Scudder's notes,' he said.

I took out the little book and began to explain the code to him. He was very quick and he knew what the names meant. We worked hard for an hour or more.

'Scudder was right about one thing,' he said. 'A French officer is coming to London on 15 June, and that's the day after tomorrow. I thought that it was all secret. Of course we know that there are a few German spies in England. We've got some of our men in Germany too. But how did they all discover the secret of this Frenchman's visit? I don't believe Scudder's story about war and the Black Stone. He always had some strange ideas.'

Sir Walter stood up again and walked about the room. 'The Black Stone,' he repeated. '*Der Schwarzestein*. It's like something out of a cheap story, isn't it? I don't believe the part about Karolides either. He's an important man, but nobody wants to kill him. Perhaps Scudder heard about some danger, but it isn't very important. It's the usual spy business, which the Germans enjoy very much. Sometimes they kill a man in the way that they killed Scudder. And the German government pays them for it.'

The butler came into the room.

'It's the telephone, sir,' he said. 'Your office in London. Mr Heath wants to speak to you.'

Sir Walter left the library. When he returned a few minutes later, he looked quite pale.

'Scudder was right,' he said, 'and I was wrong. Karolides is dead. He was shot about three hours ago.'

Chapter 8   The Black Stone

In the morning the butler took away the dinner-suit and gave me some other clothes. I went down to breakfast and found Sir Walter at the table. There was a telegram in his hand.

'I was busy last night,' he said. 'I spoke to the Foreign Secretary and to the Secretary for War. They telephoned the First Lord of the Admiralty, and they're bringing the Frenchman to London today, not tomorrow. His name's Royer, and he'll be here at five o'clock this evening. This telegram is from the First Lord of the Admiralty.'

He offered me the hot food on the table, and I began to eat. It was a very good breakfast.

'I don't think that this change is going to help us,' he continued. 'Our enemies discovered the first date, so they'll probably discover the new one too. There has to be a German spy in the Foreign Office or in the War Office. Only five men knew that Royer was coming. That's what we believed, at least. But someone told Scudder and the Germans.'

'Can't you change your plans for war?' I asked.

'We can but we don't want to. We've thought a lot about these plans and they're the best possible ones.'

'But if it's necessary, you will change them.'

'Perhaps. It's a difficult problem, Hannay. Our enemies aren't children. They're not going to steal any papers from Royer. They want to know our plans, but they want to get them in secret. Then Royer will go back to France and say, "Here are the British plans for war, and they're completely secret. The Germans don't know anything about them."'

'Then you'll have to give the Frenchman special protection,' I said. 'Someone who will stay by his side all the time.'

'Royer is having dinner with the Foreign Secretary tonight. Then he's coming to my house, where he'll meet four people.

They are Sir Arthur Drew, General Winstanley, Mr Whittaker and me. The First Lord isn't well, so Whittaker is coming in his place. And he's bringing the plans from the First Lord's office at the Admiralty. We'll take them to Royer, who will then leave for Portsmouth. A warship is waiting there to take him to France. He'll have special protection all the time.'

After breakfast we left for London by car.

Sir Walter said, 'I'm taking you to Scotland Yard, Hannay. I want you to meet the Chief of Police.'

It was half past eleven when we reached Scotland Yard. We walked into the great dark building, and I met the Chief of Police. His name was MacGillivray.

'I've brought you the murderer,' Sir Walter said.

The Chief smiled. 'I'll be very happy when you bring me the real murderer, Bullivant. Good morning, Mr Hannay. You interest us greatly.'

'And he's going to tell you some interesting things,' Sir Walter said, 'but not today. You have to wait for twenty-four hours, I'm afraid. Mr Hannay is a free man now, isn't he?'

'Yes, of course,' the Chief of Police said. Then he turned to me. 'Do you want to go back to your old flat? It's ready for you, but perhaps you'd like to move to a different home.'

I was thinking about Scudder and could not reply.

'Well,' Sir Walter said, 'I have to go now. Perhaps we'll need some of your men, MacGillivray, tonight or tomorrow. There will probably be some trouble.'

When we were leaving, Sir Walter took my hand.

'You're all right now, Hannay,' he said. 'You'll be quite safe in London. Come and see me tomorrow. But don't talk about these spies, will you? It's best to stay in your flat today.' He laughed suddenly. 'If these Black Stone people see you, they'll kill you.'

When Sir Walter had left, I felt quite alone. I was a free man, and everything was all right. But I was very nervous. I went to the Savoy Hotel and ordered a fine meal. But I did not enjoy it. People were looking at me, and I thought, 'Do they know me? Did they see my photograph in the newspapers?' I soon left the hotel.

In the afternoon I got a taxi and drove several kilometres to North London. I paid the taxi-driver and then began to walk back. I walked for hours and at last came to the centre of London again. I was feeling very unhappy. It was six o'clock, and important things were taking place in London. Royer was already there. Sir Walter was busy at the Foreign Office or making plans for the meeting. The Black Stone spies were watching and waiting quietly. But what was I doing? I was walking around the centre of London.

Suddenly a strange thought came into my head. I believed that there was great danger in London that day. And I was suddenly sure that only I could fight against it. But what could I do? Sir Walter did not need me. I could not walk into a meeting of important officers and Ministers. I could look for the German spies, of course. I was quite sure of one thing: my country needed me in this time of trouble. I had to destroy their plans; the German spies must not win.

'But is that true, Hannay?' I said to myself. 'Can't Sir Walter and his friends easily look after Britain? Doesn't the First Lord of the Admiralty know his business better than you do? Can a few German spies do anything against all of them?'

I was not sure. There was a little voice in my ear which repeated again and again: 'Do something, Hannay. Get up and do something now. If you don't, you'll never sleep well again.'

At half past nine I was walking along Jermyn Street. And I decided what to do. I decided to go to Sir Walter's house. I knew the address and I could easily find it. He did not want to see me, but I had to do something.

I came to Duke Street and walked past a group of young men.

They were wearing dinner-suits and were leaving a hotel. One of the young men was Mr Marmaduke Jopley. He saw me.

'Look!' he cried. 'It's the murderer! Hold him! Hold him! That's Hannay the murderer!'

Jopley caught my arm, and the others hurried to help him. A policeman ran across the street. I hit Jopley hard with my left hand and saw him fall. But then the crowd held me and I could not move.

'What's the matter here?' the policeman said.

'That's Hannay, the murderer,' Jopley shouted.

'Oh, be quiet,' I said. 'I'm not a murderer. Listen, officer. Don't arrest me. The Chief of Police knows all about me. I was at Scotland Yard this morning.'

'Now young man, come along with me,' the policeman said. 'I saw you begin this fight.' He looked at Jopley, who was lying on the ground. 'That man didn't do anything to you, but I saw you hit him. Now come along quietly to the police station.'

I was very angry. I heard the little voice in my ear again. 'You have to get away,' it said. 'Don't spend another minute here.'

Suddenly I felt very strong. I turned quickly and threw the policeman to the ground. I pushed the other men away and ran along Duke Street.

I can run very fast when I want to. And that evening I almost flew. In a few minutes I reached Pall Mall and turned towards St James's Park. I ran between the taxis in the Mall and across the bridge. There were very few people in the park and nobody stopped me. Sir Walter's house was at Queen Anne's Gate and there I began to walk.

Three or four cars were standing in the street outside the house. I walked up to the door and pushed the bell. The butler opened the door. I could hear cries far away, but the street was empty.

'I have to see Sir Walter,' I said. 'My business is very important.'

I hit Jopley hard with my left hand and saw him fall.

'Come in, sir,' he said. 'I'm afraid you can't see him now. But you can wait in the hall until the meeting finishes.'

It was an old house with a large square hall. Doors led into several rooms on each side. An officer who was dressed in plain clothes stood outside one of the doors. I sat down in a corner near the telephone.

I made a sign to the butler. 'I'm in trouble again,' I said. 'But I'm working for Sir Walter, and he knows all about it. The police and a crowd of people are following me. If they come here, please don't let them come in. And don't tell them that I'm here.'

'All right, sir,' he replied.

A minute or two later I heard voices outside. Then came the sound of the door-bell, and the butler went to answer it. Someone spoke to him from outside, and he suddenly stood up very straight.

'I am sorry,' he said. 'This is Sir Walter Bullivant's house, and Sir Walter is Chief Secretary at the Foreign Office. I'm afraid that I don't know anything about a murderer. Now please go away, or I shall call the police myself.'

Then he shut the door and walked back through the hall.

Two minutes later I heard the bell again, and a man came in. While he was taking off his coat, I saw his face. It was a famous face, and I knew it from his photographs in the newspapers. The man was Lord Alloa, the First Lord of the Admiralty. He was a big man with a large nose and sharp blue eyes. He walked past me, and the plain clothes officer opened the door of the room for him.

I waited in the hall for twenty minutes. And during this time the little voice continued to speak in my ear. 'Don't go away,' it said. 'They'll soon need you.' A little bell went at the back of the house and the butler came into the hall. The First Lord left the meeting room, and the butler gave him his coat. I looked at the man for a moment, and he looked straight at me. It was all very

I looked at the man for a moment, and he looked straight at me.

fast. My heart jumped suddenly because I saw a light in his eyes. I did not know the First Lord, and he did not know me. But I was quite sure about that sudden light in his eyes. It meant that he knew my face. He looked away and walked to the door. The butler opened it for him and closed it behind him.

I picked up the telephone book and quickly found Lord Alloa's number. His butler answered.

'Is the First Lord at home?' I asked.

'Yes, sir,' the voice said. 'But he's not very well. He's in bed. Can I give him a message, sir?'

'No, thank you,' I said, and I put the telephone down.

I walked quickly across the hall and entered the meeting room. Five surprised faces looked up from a round table. Sir Walter was there and Drew, the War Minister. Sir Arthur Drew's photograph was often in the papers. I already knew General Winstanley. An older man, who was probably Whittaker, stood next to him. The fifth man was short and fat.

Sir Walter looked quite angry.

'This is Mr Hannay,' he said. 'I've already told you something about him. But why have you come here, Hannay? You know that we're very busy.'

'Your enemies are busy too, sir,' I said. 'And one of them has just left this room.'

Sir Walter's face grew red as he said, 'But that was Lord Alloa.'

'It was not,' I cried. 'Lord Alloa is at home in bed. I have just spoken to his butler on the telephone. The man who was here knew my face. And Lord Alloa doesn't know me.'

'Then – who – who–?' someone asked.

'The Black Stone,' I cried. I looked around the table and saw fear in five pairs of eyes.

Chapter 9   The Thirty-nine Steps

'But that can't be true,' Mr Whittaker said. 'Lord Alloa told me that he was probably not going to come to the meeting. But I know him very well and was not surprised to see him here. You're quite wrong about this, Hannay.'

Sir Walter left the room and spoke to someone on the telephone. When he came back, his face had turned pale.

'I've spoken to Alloa,' he said. 'He got out of bed to come to the telephone. Hannay is right. That man was not Lord Alloa.'

'I don't believe it,' General Winstanley said. 'Alloa was standing next to me ten minutes ago.'

'Gentlemen,' I said, 'the Black Stone knows its business. You probably didn't look at the man very well. You were talking about these important plans. The man looked like Lord Alloa, and so you accepted him. But it was another man, and I probably saw him in Scotland.'

Then the Frenchman spoke. 'This young man is right,' he said slowly. 'Our enemies know their business very well. Listen and I'll tell you a true story. Many years ago, I was in Senegal. I was living in a hotel but every day I went fishing. The river was a few kilometres away and I rode there on a little horse.

'Well, one day I packed my lunch as usual and hung it over the horse's neck. Then I left for the river. When I arrived there, I tied the horse to a tree. I fished for several hours, and I was thinking only about the fish. I didn't look at the horse at all, but I could hear her. And I could see her shape out of the corner of my eye. She was moving about a lot and making a bit of noise too. I spoke to her as usual, but I did not look up from the water.

'Well, lunchtime came, so I put the fish into a bag and walked along the river bank. While I was walking, I continued to watch the water. When I reached the tree, I threw the bag on to the horse's back . . .'

The Frenchman stopped and looked around the table.

'It was the smell that hit me first. I looked up and turned my head. My bag was lying on a lion's back. The horse was dead and half eaten on the ground behind him.'

'What did you do?' I asked. I knew that this was a real African story.

'I shot the lion in the head,' he said. 'But before he died, he took a part of me.' And he held up his left hand, which only had two fingers on it.

'That horse died hours before I finished fishing,' he continued. 'And the lion was watching me all the time. He was a brown shape near the tree. I saw the shape and colour but I did not really look at him. That was my mistake, gentlemen, and we have made the same mistake tonight.'

Sir Walter agreed.

'This Black Stone man,' the General said, 'is he a German spy or something? Nobody could keep all these facts in his head. It doesn't seem very important to me.'

'Oh, yes, he could,' the Frenchman replied. 'A good spy can remember everything. His eyes are like a camera. Do you remember that he didn't speak at all? He read the papers several times but didn't say anything. You can be sure that he has all the facts now. When I was young, I could do the same thing.'

'Well, we'll have to change the plans,' Sir Walter said.

Mr Whittaker looked surprised. 'Did you say that to Lord Alloa?' he asked.

'No.'

'Of course we can't decide it now. But I'm almost sure about this: if we change the plans, we'll have to change the coast of England too!'

'And there's another problem,' Royer said. 'I've told you some of the French plans, and that German spy heard them. Now we can't possibly change our plans. But we *can* do this, gentlemen:

we can catch them before they leave the country.'

'But how?' I cried. 'We don't know anything about them.'

'And there's the post,' Whittaker said. 'They can easily send the facts to Germany by post. Perhaps they are on their way there now. We can't possibly search the post.'

'No,' the Frenchman said. 'You don't know how a good spy works. He carries the secrets himself. The Germans will pay the man who brings the plans. So we have a chance. The man has to get across the sea to reach Germany, and we'll have to search all ships. Believe me, gentlemen. This matter is very important for both France and Britain.'

Royer was clearly an intelligent man, and he had the right ideas. But where could we find these German spies? The problem was a very difficult one. Then I remembered Scudder's book.

'Sir Walter,' I cried, 'did you bring Scudder's notebook from the cottage? I've just remembered something in it.'

He went to a cupboard. And a few moments later I found the page.

'*Thirty-nine steps*,' I read. '*Thirty-nine steps. I counted them. High tide is at 10.17 p.m.*'

Whittaker was looking at me. 'What does all that mean?' he asked.

'Scudder knew these spies,' I said. 'And he knew the place where they lived. They're probably leaving the country tomorrow. And I believe that we'll find them near the sea. There are steps at this place, and it has a high tide at seventeen minutes past ten.'

'But they will probably leave tonight,' someone said. 'They won't wait until tomorrow.'

'I don't think so. They have their own secret way and they're not going to hurry. They're Germans, aren't they? And Germans always like to follow a plan. Now where can we find a book of tides?'

'Well, it's a chance,' Whittaker said, 'and it's probably our only chance to catch them.'

'Isn't there a book of tides at the Admiralty?' Sir Walter asked.

'Yes, of course,' Whittaker replied. 'Let's go there now.'

We went out into the hall, and the butler gave the gentlemen their coats. We got into two of the cars, but Sir Walter did not come with us.

'I'm going to Scotland Yard,' he said. 'We'll probably need some of MacGillivray's men.'

We reached the Admiralty and followed Whittaker through several empty rooms to the map room. There he found a book of tides and gave it to me. I sat down at a desk and the others stood around me. But the job was too difficult for any of us. There were hundreds of names in the book. And high tide was at seventeen minutes past ten in forty or fifty places.

I put down the book and began to think about the steps.

'We're looking for a place,' I said, 'which probably has several staircases. But the important one has thirty-nine steps.'

'And the tide is important too,' Royer said. 'So that means that it's probably a small port. These people won't try to get away in a big boat. They may have a small sailing boat or a fishing boat.'

'That's quite possible,' I said. 'The place may not be a port at all. These spies were in London, and now they want to go to Germany. So they'll probably leave from a place on the East Coast.'

I picked up a piece of paper and wrote down our ideas.

1 The place has several staircases. The important one has thirty-nine steps.
2 High tide is at seventeen minutes past ten. High tide is necessary for the boat to leave.
3 The place is a small port or perhaps a piece of open coast.
4 The Germans may use a sailing boat or a fishing boat.

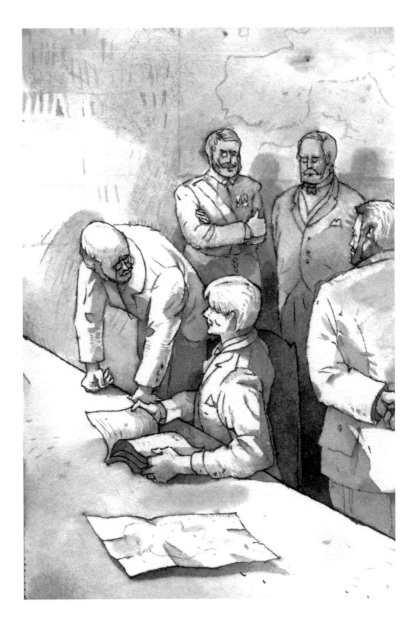

I sat down at a desk and the others stood around me.

Then I made three guesses and wrote them down:

1 The place is a piece of open coast.
2 The boat is probably small and foreign.
3 The place is on the East Coast between Cromer and Dover.

Sir Walter came into the room with MacGillivray behind him.

'The police are watching the ports and railway stations,' MacGillivray said. 'But it's not going to be easy for them. They're looking for a fat man, a thin man and an old man!'

I showed my paper to Sir Walter and said, 'These are our ideas. But we'll need someone to help us.' I turned to Whittaker and said, 'Is there a Chief Coastguard on the East Coast?'

'I don't know. But I know one in London. He lives in Clapham and he knows the East Coast very well.'

'Can you bring him here tonight?' I asked.

'Yes, I think so. I'll go to his house.'

It was very late when Whittaker returned with the coastguard. He was a fine old man and very polite to the officers. Sir Arthur Drew spoke to him first.

'We're looking for a place on the East Coast,' he said, 'where there are several staircases. The steps probably lead down to a beach. Do you know any place like that?'

'Well, sir, I don't know. There's Brattlesham in Norfolk, of course. There are steps there, but only the fishermen use them.'

'That isn't the place,' I said.

'Then there are a lot of holiday places. They usually have a few steps.'

'No. This is probably a very quiet place.'

'Then I'm sorry, gentlemen. I don't know. There's only the Ruff—'

'What's that?' I asked.

'It's a bit of high ground on the Kent coast. Near Bradgate.

There are some fine houses on the top and some of them have steps down to the beach. They're private beaches, of course.'

'What do you mean by that?'

'Well, the people who own the houses also own the beaches, sir. When you buy a house there, you get a piece of private beach as well.'

I picked up the book of tides and found Bradgate. High tide there was at twenty-seven minutes past ten on 15 June.

'How can I find the time of high tide at the Ruff?' I asked the coastguard.

'Oh, I know that, sir. I stayed there once in June. It's ten minutes before high tide at Bradgate.'

I shut the book and looked around.

'Sir Walter,' I said, 'can I borrow your car and a map of the roads in Kent? I'd like to have some of your men too, MacGillivray. Perhaps we can surprise these Germans tomorrow morning.'

They did not answer me for a moment. I did not work for the Foreign Office or the Admiralty, or the General. But I was young and strong and I already knew these spies.

It was Royer who spoke first. 'I'm quite happy,' he said, 'to leave this matter in Mr Hannay's hands.'

Sir Walter said, 'I think so too.' And MacGillivray agreed.

Half an hour later I was driving quickly through the villages of Kent. MacGillivray's best officer was sitting next to me in the car. It was half past three in the morning.

Chapter 10   The House by the Sea

We stayed at the Griffin Hotel in Bradgate. At seven o'clock in the morning I was looking out of a window there. It was a beautiful day. A man was fishing down at the port, and I

65

remembered Royer's story about the lion.

A small warship was lying south of the port. I called MacGillivray's man.

'Officer,' I said, 'do you know that ship? Perhaps Whittaker sent her here.'

'I don't think so,' he said. 'She's usually along this part of the coast.' And he told me her name and the name of her captain. I went to the telephone and sent a telegram to Sir Walter about them.

After breakfast Scaife, MacGillivray's officer, and I walked along the beach. We went towards the steps on the Ruff but stopped less than half a kilometre from them.

'I won't come all the way with you,' I said. 'These people know me very well. I'll wait here. You go on and count all the steps.'

I sat down behind a rock and waited. There was nobody on the beach. It was ten o'clock when Scaife came back.

'There are six lots of steps,' he said, 'and they lead to six different houses.' He took a piece of paper from his pocket and read: 'Thirty-four, thirty-five, thirty-nine, forty-two, forty-seven and twenty-one.'

I felt so pleased that I almost got up and shouted.

We hurried back to Bradgate and sent a telegram to MacGillivray. I wanted six good men, and they had to stay at different hotels in the town.

'Now go back to the thirty-nine steps,' I said to Scaife, 'and have a look at the house. Then go to the post office. Find out who lives there.'

He brought back some strange but interesting facts. The house was called Trafalgar Lodge and it belonged to an old man named Appleton. Mr Appleton often stayed there in the summer. He was at the house now. Nobody knew a lot about him but he seemed kind and quiet. Scaife made some excuse to visit the house and met three women there.

'They look after the place,' he said, 'and they can't possibly be Germans. They talk too much for that.'

'Did you look at the houses on each side of Trafalgar Lodge?' I asked.

'Yes. The house on the right is empty. They're building the place on the left.'

Before dinner I walked along the Ruff myself. I found a quiet place away from the houses and sat down there. I could see the house quite well. It was a red stone building with large windows. There was a garden all around the house, and the British flag was flying from a tall post!

While I was watching, a man left the house to walk along the hill-top. He was an old man wearing white trousers and a blue coat. He had a newspaper under his arm. He walked quite a long way and then sat down on a seat to read the paper. A few minutes later he put down the paper and looked out to sea at the warship. He looked at it for a long time. I watched him for half an hour, and then he got up to return to the house. I went back to my hotel.

I was not very happy about that old man. He did not look like a spy, but perhaps he was the old man from that Scottish farm.

In the afternoon we had some excitement. A sailing boat came up from the south and stopped near the Ruff. She was flying the British flag. Scaife and I went down to the port and spoke to the coastguard there. We said that we wanted to go fishing. So the coastguard got a boat for us, and we sailed out of the port.

We caught a lot of fish that afternoon. And at about four o'clock we sailed quite close to the sailing boat. She looked like a beautiful white bird on the water.

'She's a fast boat,' Scaife said. 'If anyone wants to get away quickly, they'll go in a ship like this.'

Her name was the *Ariadne*. We spoke to a few men on her, and they were clearly Englishmen. Then an officer joined them, and the men stopped talking. The officer was a young man and he spoke English very well. But we were quite sure that he was not an Englishman. His hair was cut very short and his clothes looked quite foreign.

In the evening I met the captain of the warship at the hotel.

'We'll probably need your ship tonight or tomorrow,' I said. 'Has anyone spoken to you about that?'

'Yes, sir. I've had a message from the Admiralty. I'll come in close when it's dark. I know what to do.'

About an hour later I walked back along the hill-top towards Trafalgar Lodge. The old man and a young man were playing tennis in the garden. While I was watching them, a woman brought out bottles and glasses. The young man, who was rather fat, took the things from her.

'Those people seem all right,' I said to myself. 'They're quite different from those terrible men in Scotland. I've probably made a mistake.'

Then another man arrived at the house on a bicycle. He was thin, dark and quite young. They finished the game of tennis and they all went into the house.

I walked slowly back to the hotel. Was I wrong about those men? Were they acting while I was watching them? They did not know that anyone was watching them. And they were acting like any other Englishmen.

But there *were* three men in that house: the old man, the fat one and the thin, dark man. The house fitted Scudder's description. A sailing boat was lying less than a kilometre away and she had a foreign officer. I thought about Karolides and the danger of war. And I remembered the fear in Sir Arthur Drew's face.

I knew what I had to do. I had to go to that house and arrest those men. If I was wrong, it was my problem. But I did not like the job at all.

Suddenly I remembered my friend Peter Pienaar in Rhodesia. Peter was a criminal before he became a policeman. In fact the police accepted him for that reason. He knew all the worst criminals in the country. Peter told me that he once got away from the police very easily. He put on a black coat and went to church. And he chose to sit next to a police officer. They sang together and used the same book. And the policeman did not know who Peter was! I asked him why. And Peter replied, 'Because the place and my clothes were different. He knew me in my usual clothes, in a street or at a hotel. But he could not imagine me in church or wearing a long black coat.'

These thoughts made me feel more comfortable. Our German enemies were as clever as Peter. They lived in an English house, and the British flag was flying in the garden. They used English names and played English games. Their private life was completely English, and so nobody thought twice about them.

It was now eight o'clock in the evening. I met Scaife at the hotel and gave him his orders.

'Put two men in the garden,' I said, 'and hide three others close to the windows. When I want you, I'll call.'

I was not hungry, so I went for a walk. I saw the lights on the *Ariadne* and on the warship. I sat down on a seat and waited for more than an hour.

At half past nine I went to Trafalgar Lodge. Scaife's men were in their places by now, but I did not see anyone. There were lights in the house and the windows were open. I pushed the doorbell. One of the women opened the door.

'May I speak to Mr Appleton?' I asked.

'Yes, sir. Please come in,' she said.

I had a plan. I hoped to walk straight into the house and to watch those three German faces. But when I was inside, I felt less sure of myself. I saw their hats and coats and walking sticks in the hall. There was a large clock in one corner. English pictures were hanging on the walls, and the place was like thousands of other English homes.

'Your name, sir?' the woman asked.

'Hannay. Richard Hannay.'

She went into a room and called my name. I followed just behind her, but I was too late. The three men had a moment to hide their surprise.

The old man was standing up, and he and the fat one were wearing dinner-suits. The other man was in a suit of blue cloth.

'Mr Hannay?' the old man said. 'You want to speak to me, I believe. Come into the next room, please.'

I pulled a chair towards me and sat down on it.

'You know me,' I said, 'and you know my business.'

The light was not very good in the room. But I saw that they all looked surprised.

'Perhaps we do know you,' the old man said, 'but I can't remember. I'm sorry that I don't know your business, sir. Will you please tell me?'

I thought about Peter Pienaar and said, 'This is the end. I've come to arrest you all.'

'Arrest us!' the old man said. 'But why?'

'I'm arresting you for the murder of Franklin Scudder in London on 23 May.'

'I don't know that name,' the old man said, and his voice seemed very weak.

The fat man spoke then. 'I read about that in the papers. But this is terrible. We don't know anything about the murder, sir. Where do you come from?'

'Scotland Yard,' I said.

There was a silence when they heard that. The old man looked down at his feet and seemed very nervous.

Then the fat man said, 'This is surely a mistake, uncle. We can easily prove our stories. I wasn't even in England on 23 May, and you were ill, weren't you, Bob? You were in London, uncle, I know; but you can explain your business there.'

'That's right, Percy! Now what did I do on 23 May? Oh, I remember. I came up in the morning from Woking and had dinner with Charlie Symons. I was at Grantham House in the afternoon, wasn't I? Yes, that's right. And I stayed there all evening.'

The fat man looked at me. 'I'm afraid you've made a mistake, sir. We'll help you if we can, of course. But sometimes Scotland Yard is wrong.'

'Yes, of course,' the old man said. 'We'll do anything to help you, sir, but this is clearly a mistake.'

'Won't Nellie laugh when she hears about this!' one of them said.

'Oh, she will! I can't wait to tell Charlie about it too. Now, Mr Hannay, I'm not angry with you, but you've come to the wrong place.'

Surely they weren't acting. What they said was all true. It *was* my mistake. And I wanted to say, 'I'm sorry,' and leave the house.

But the old man had very little hair. The fat man was there too, and the third man was dark and thin. I looked at them and I looked around the room. Everything was all right and in its place. And I did not know their faces.

'Don't you agree, sir?' the old man asked me. 'Haven't you come to the wrong house?'

'No. This is the right house.'

'Well, we have other things to do with our time,' the thin man said. 'Are you going to take us to the police station? You're only doing your job, I know, but it's very difficult.'

I did not answer him. I thought, 'Oh, Peter Pienaar, help me!'

The fat man stood up. 'Perhaps Mr Hannay needs more time,'

he said. 'It isn't an easy problem for him. Let's play cards for half an hour, shall we? Do you play, sir?'

'Yes. I've got a lot of time and I like a game of cards.' We went into the next room, and I looked around. Books and newspapers were lying around. The tennis things were in an open cupboard in the corner.

We sat around a card-table in the middle of the room. And the dark man brought me a drink. I played with him against the others.

It was like a dream. The windows were open, and I could see the moonlight on the sea. The three men were not afraid at all. They were talking and laughing together. But my heart was beating very quickly.

I did not play very well that night. My thoughts were too ugly for me to follow the cards. I was not sure about these men, and they knew it of course. I looked at their faces again and again but did not know them. They did not only seem different. I felt sure that they *were* different. 'Oh, Peter,' I thought once more.

Then suddenly I saw something. The old man put down his cards to drink some wine. And he did not pick them up for a moment. He sat back in his chair and began to play with his right ear. I remembered that Scottish farm. I was standing in front of him again after telling him my story. And, there, in Scotland, he sat back and played with his ear. It was only a little thing, but I remembered it well.

The clouds lifted from my eyes and everything was clear again. The faces of the three men changed suddenly and I knew all their secrets. It was the dark man who killed Scudder. I was playing cards with him, but his eyes looked cold and hard now. The fat man was different too. He did not have one face but a hundred faces. And he was probably the Lord Alloa of the night before. But the old man was clearly the chief criminal. He was as hard as rock and quite without fear. I remembered Scudder's

We sat around a card-table in the middle of the room.

words: 'If you see his eyes, Hannay, you'll never forget them.' And it was true.

We continued to play, but my heart was full of hate. When the dark man spoke to me, I could not answer him.

'Bob! Look at the clock,' the old man said. 'You'll miss your train if we don't hurry.' He turned to me. 'Bob has to go back to London tonight.' The voice was now as completely false as their faces.

'I'm sorry,' I said, 'but he isn't going tonight.'

'Why not?' the young man asked. 'I *have* to go. I'll give you my address.'

'No. You have to stay here.'

That probably made them nervous. They knew that I knew them. They had only one chance now, and the old man took it.

'Well, arrest me, Mr Hannay, and let the others go. Will that be all right?'

I shouted, 'Scaife!'

The lights went out. Strong arms held me, and I could not move.

'*Schnell, Franz,*' a voice cried, '*zum Boot, zum Boot!*'

I looked out of the window. Two police officers were running across the garden. The dark man jumped through the window and was running towards the steps. Suddenly the room filled with people, and I was free. I caught the old man and held him. Scaife and another policeman fell on the fat one. The lights came on.

We looked out of the window again. Franz reached the steps before the policemen. He opened the gate, which locked itself behind him. And the policemen could not follow. We waited for a few minutes.

Suddenly the old man was free again. He hurried to the wall of the room and pushed something. A great noise rose up from below the house. The steps flew into the air.

'Dynamite!' I cried. 'They've destroyed the stairs!'

A great noise rose up from below the house. The steps flew into the air.

The old man was looking at me and laughing. A terrible light burned in his eyes.

'He is safe,' he shouted. 'You cannot follow him. He has gone . . . He has won. *Der schwarze Stein ist in der Siegesthrone!*'

Two police officers caught the old man by the arms, and I said my last words to him.

'Franz hasn't won anything. He'll reach the *Ariadne* quite safely, I'm sure. But she was in our hands an hour ago.'

Everyone knows that the war began early in August 1914. That was about six weeks after I helped to catch those three German spies. I was an officer during those unhappy war years. But perhaps my best work was done before it started.

ACTIVITIES

Chapters 1–2

Before you read

1 What do you know about the First World War? Find out:
    a when it started.
    b when it finished.
    c which countries fought in it.

2 Look at the Word List at the back of the book. Which are words:
    a for people?   **c** for buildings?
    b about the sea?

While you read

3 Are these sentences about Hannay (H) or Scudder (S)?
    a He has a lot of money. .....
    b He knows dangerous secrets. .....
    c His enemies are waiting for him. .....
    d He never leaves the flat. .....
    e He dies. .....
    f A milkman helps him. .....

After you read

4 Why:
    a is Scudder afraid?
    b does Hannay not call the police?
    Who:
    c can stop the war?
    d has unforgettable eyes?
    What:
    e does Hannay find in his tobacco box?
    f does Hannay not have time to do?
    How:
    g does Scudder die?
    h does Hannay escape from Scudder's enemies?

5 Work with another student. Have this conversation between Hannay and a friend.

Student A: You are Hannay. Tell your friend about Scudder and why you plan to go to Scotland.

Student B: You are Hannay's friend. You don't like Hannay's plans. You think that he should go straight to the police. Tell him why.

Chapters 3–4

Before you read

6 Discuss these questions. What do you think? What will:

a Hannay do in Scotland?

b the milkman do in London?

c the police do when they find Scudder's body?

d Scudder's enemies do?

While you read

7 In which order does Hannay see or meet these people? Number them, 1–7.

a a man in a plane .....

b three men talking to railwaymen .....

c an old man with a dog .....

d a politician .....

e a husband and wife .....

f an innkeeper .....

g a policeman with a telegram .....

h a farmer .....

After you read

8 Is Hannay happy to meet or see the people in Question 7? Why (not)?

9 Why are these people or things important in these chapters?

a a newspaper **b** a dog **c** Julia Czechenyi

d the plan to kill Karolides **e** a French officer

f the Black Stone **g** Mr Twisdon

10 Is Hannay right to do these things? Why (not)? Discuss your ideas with another student.

    a He jumps off the train.

    b He gives the innkeeper a torn piece of paper.

    c He steals a car.

    d He tells the innkeeper and Sir Harry about his problem.

    e He makes a speech in a town hall.

    f He decides to stay in Scotland until 12 or 13 June.

11 Work with another student. Have this conversation between a policeman and the milkman.

    Student A: You are the policeman. You do not believe the milkman's story. You think that he murdered Scudder. Say why.

    Student B: Tell the policeman about Hannay. Tell him why you are not a murderer.

Chapters 5–6

Before you read

12 Discuss these questions.

    a Why is 15 June an important day?

    b What does Hannay plan to do between now and 15 June?

While you read

13 Circle the correct words.

    a Hannay throws away his bicycle because he sees a *car/plane*.

    b The men in the car think that Hannay's *glasses/shoes* are strange.

    c Marmaduke Jopley thinks that Hannay is *crazy/dangerous*.

    d *The police/Hannay's enemies* are searching the long grass.

    e The old man in the glass building *has Scudder's notebook/is Hannay's main enemy*.

    f The old man does not kill Hannay because he does not want *the police to come/to kill the wrong man*.

    g Hannay discovers a secret *airfield/message*.

After you read

14 How are these people or things useful to Hannay?

    a the roadman   **b** an old friend in Rhodesia

    c Marmaduke Jopley   **d** the old man in the glass building

    e dirty clothes   **f** dynamite and detonators

    g a stone bird house

15 Which words describe Hannay in these chapters? Why?

    angry   dishonest   drunk   happy   hungry   lucky   nervous

    sad   sick and thirsty   weak like a child

16 Work with another student. Have this conversation between the man with strange eyes and another foreign spy.

    Student A: You are the man with strange eyes. You do not want to kill Hannay yet. Explain why.

    Student B: You are another foreign spy. You want to kill Hannay now. Explain why.

Chapters 7–8

Before you read

17 Discuss these questions. What do you think?

    a How is Hannay feeling now?

    b What does he look like?

    c How is he going to get away from his enemies?

While you read

18 Are these sentences right (✓) or wrong (✗)?

    a Hannay stays for ten days at Turnbull's cottage because he is afraid of his foreign enemies.   .....

    b Sir Walter Bullivant is surprised by Hannay's visit.   .....

    c The police know that Hannay is not a murderer.   .....

    d Sir Walter does not believe Scudder's story at first.   .....

    e Hannay is invited to a meeting at Sir Walter's London house.   .....

    f A policeman tries to arrest Hannay for Scudder's murder.   .....

    g The First Lord of the Admiralty is a spy.   .....

19 There are six mistakes in this description of Hannay's activities in this chapter. What are they?

After his illness, Hannay goes to London to see Sir Walter Bullivant, Marmaduke Jopley's uncle. Sir Walter tells him that Scudder's ideas were often right. After news of the Greek Prime Minister's death, Sir Walter goes to an important meeting. Hannay meets Marmaduke Jopley. Jopley hits Hannay and Hannay runs to Sir Walter's office at Queen Anne's Gate. Sir Walter and his other guests are surprised that a foreign spy has stolen their secret plans.

20 Finish these sentences.

  a Hannay goes back to Turnbull's cottage because ...

  b Turnbull is rude to Hannay because ...

  c Hannay sings "Annie Laurie" because ...

  d Sir Walter changes his mind about Scudder's story because ...

  e Hannay is unhappy in London because ...

  f Hannay telephones Lord Alloa's number because ....

  g The men at the meeting look frightened because ...

21 Discuss these statements with another student. Do you agree with them? Why (not)?

  a The best spies always work with other spies.

  b Karolides died because of the mistakes of Scudder, Hannay and Sir Walter Bullivant.

  c The German spies are better at their job than the British spies.

Chapters 9–10

Before you read

22 Discuss these questions. What do you think?

  a Who was the man with Lord Alloa's face?

  b Why are the thirty-nine steps important?

  c What will the Black Stone spies do next?

23 Find the right endings to these sentences.

a	Lord Alloa is still in	Senegal.
b	Royer tells a story about	Germany.
c	MacGillivray works at	Sir Walter's house.
d	The map room is in	Scotland Yard.
e	Hannay guesses that the spies will go to	Scotland.
f	The thirty-nine steps are near	the East Coast.
g	The spies live in	the Admiralty.
h	The spies plan to escape to	Trafalgar House.
i	The night before, the fat spy was at	Bradgate, Kent.

After you read

24 Only one of these sentences is right. Which one? Correct the others.

a Royer lost some fingers in a fishing accident.

b The spies have already posted their secrets to Germany.

c Hannay thinks that the spies will try to escape in a warship from a small port on the East Coast.

d Hannay and the others discover the thirty-nine steps with the help of a coastguard who lives in London.

e Scaife and Hannay go fishing in the sea because they do not want the spies to see them near their house.

f Hannay thinks that the people in Trafalgar House look like the enemy spies in Scotland.

g The old spy with the strange eyes killed Scudder, and the thin spy was probably the Lord Alloa of the night before.

h At the end of the story, one of the spies escapes to Germany.

25 Work with another student. Have this conversation between the British Prime Minister and Sir Walter Bullivant.

Student A: You are the Prime Minister. You are angry with Sir Walter because too many things went wrong. Tell him why you are angry.

Student B: You are Sir Walter. You think that the Foreign Office did a good job. Tell the Prime Minister why he should not be angry.

Writing

26 When he is on a train, Hannay reads about the milkman in a newspaper. Write the newspaper story. Start like this: MURDER IN A LONDON FLAT

27 Imagine that you are Hannay. Write a letter to the roadman. Thank him for his help. Tell him your real reason for doing his job.

28 Write a description of Richard Hannay. What do you know about him? What does he look like? What does he do? What is he like?

29 You work for a Scottish holiday company. Write about Galloway for a holiday magazine. Why is it a perfect place for a holiday?

30 You are Sir Harry in Chapter 4. Your uncle wants more information about Mr Twisdon. Write a full description of your day from the time you nearly crash into Hannay's car until two o'clock the next morning. What sort of man is Twisdon? How do know? Why should your uncle help him?

31 Imagine that you are the old spy with strange eyes. How did you know where Scudder lived? How was Scudder killed? How did you know that Hannay was in Scotland? Why did you have a house in Scotland *and* a house in Kent? How and why was the Greek Prime Minister killed? Why were you working for the Germans? Write *your* side of the story!

32 Do you find this story believable? Which parts do you find least believable? Write about them and give your reasons.

33 'A good spy must be a good actor.' Write about the importance of 'acting' in this story.

34 Work with another student. Think of a simple code. Write a message in this code. Give your coded message to your friend. Who can read the message first?

35 Royer says that good spies never send secrets by post. Sir Walter Bullivant says that good spies never work alone. Write an introduction for a book about spies. Think of five or six more things that good spies should / should not do. Give your reasons.

WORD LIST

admiralty (n) the government office that looks after a country's ships

arrest (v) to catch someone and take them to a police station

butler (n) a man who looks after the needs of a rich employer at home

captain (n) the chief officer on a ship

coastguard (n) a person or group of people that helps boats or swimmers in danger

code (n) a secret way of sending messages in words, letters or signs

cottage (n) a small house in the country

detonator (n) a piece of equipment that lights dynamite

dynamite (n) something that can destroy buildings and walls of rock. When you light it, it makes a very loud noise.

general (n) a very important soldier; one of the highest officers

innkeeper (n) a person who looks after a small hotel, usually with a bar, in the country

lion (n) a large wild cat found in Africa and Asia

lord (n) a man with a high position because of the family that he comes from

politics (n) ideas about government; government activities

minister (n) one of the most important people in the government in many countries which have a parliament; the most important of them is the **prime minister**

Sir (n) a title given to a man by the government for his work

telegram (n) a short written message sent by electrical signs

tide (n) the movement of the sea towards and away from the coast

tobacco (n) pieces from a dried brown plant that are smoked in pipes and cigarettes

town hall (n) a building used for the government of a town

A Scandal in Bohemia
Sir Arthur Conan Doyle

All kinds of people, from shopkeepers to kings, want the help of
Sherlock Holmes in these six stories about the adventures of the
famous detective. Who put a diamond in a chicken? Why is there
a club for men with red hair? How did the man at the lake die? Can
Sherlock Holmes solve the mysteries?

The No.1 Ladies' Detective Agency
Alexander McCall Smith

Precious Ramotswe is a kind, warm hearted and large African
lady. She is also the only female private detective in Botswana.
Her agency – the No. 1 Ladies' Detective Agency – is the best
in the country. With the help of her secretary, Mma Makutsi, and
her best friend, Mr JLB Matekoni, she solves a number of difficult
– and sometimes dangerous – problems. A missing husband, a
missing finger and a missing child – she will solve these mysteries
in her own special way.

K's First Case
L.G. Alexander

Sir Michael Gray is the victim of a murder and he was very rich.
Katrina Kirby – or K as she is called – is a detective and she wants
to find out who the murderer is. But there are lots of suspects. This
is K's first case. Can you help her find the murderer?

*There are hundreds of Penguin Readers to choose from – world classics,
film adaptations, modern-day crime and adventure, short stories,
biographies, American classics, non-fiction, plays ...*

For a complete list of all Penguin Readers titles, please contact your local
Pearson Longman office or visit our website.

www.penguinreaders.com